THESE THINGS
REMAIN

CARLYLE MARNEY

THESE THINGS REMAIN

ABINGDON-COKESBURY
New York
Nashville • PRESS

THESE THINGS REMAIN

Copyright MCMLIII by Pierce & Washabaugh

Library of Congress Catalog Card Number: 53-5398

SET UP, PRINTED, AND BOUND BY THE
PARTHENON PRESS, AT NASHVILLE,
TENNESSEE, UNITED STATES OF AMERICA

TO MY FATHER,
whose God I also serve

PREFACE

SOMETIMES, IN A HAPPY REVERSAL OF THE ORDINARY, congregations exhaust the preacher. When the big bell in near-by St. Mary's sounds down our street on Sunday mornings, it says, "Five of twelve and you ought to be done." Usually I am—completely done, emptied by the pull of the most expectant congregation a man could pray to serve. Every conceivable human need alongside every human glory sits there—hoping for some authentic word from God. Most times it must exhaust the congregation too.

Only an unfeeling dolt could fail to be stirred by that crossroads meeting of spirits—my own congregation—for whom these messages were first prepared. If these pages sing of eternal things, it is because this congregation matters—eternally. I see them as I read these words my heart could not refuse to cry, to some from the over-shadowing university, to some from under the capitol dome, and to many from the avenue. Ph.D. and shopgirl, owner and day laborer, veteran professor and little child—on common ground, sharing the proclamation.

And, too, I see here and there faces of those Cross veterans to whom I can never be pastor—they long ago left me behind along "the Way," singing and shouting their victory won before the war is over.

7

THESE THINGS REMAIN

In joy at the triumph of their spirits these soundings of my own spirit travail are flung out to fellow travelers—pilgrims all and, like me, sinners too.

Carlyle Marney

CONTENTS

THESE THINGS REMAIN

The Gospel in Christ
for Every Man

CHAPTER ONE

But how can he escape the pattern?
How can he get out of what drudgery and the
    everydayness of every day will do to him?
Nothing he does endures after payday.
    Nothing he thinks has consequence.
        Nothing he says matters.
            All he sees decays.
            All he loves dies.
        All he wants disappears.

How can he escape unless he
finds something that endures?

All tangibles perish; time gets
everything, and men are caught.

*Does nothing endure? Is there
that that remains, and can a
man get it for himself, and
for his fellows?*

THESE THINGS REMAIN

I

TOMORROW MORNING YOUR ALARM CLOCK WILL GO OFF about three hours too early. You will grumble, turn over, reach for it, shut it off, grumble some more, fight your way out, and put on something to go to work in. You will eat too much fat and sugar, not enough protein; you will eat it too fast, too taut and tied up; and as soon as you have swallowed the last bite, you'll call for any to hear, "I'm gone!"

You will catch your ride, or your bus, or fight for a parking place; and another day will be upon you. On your way to town you will have developed heartburn from having hurried too much, from having eaten the wrong things too fast; so you'll take a Tum or soothe it with some patented foaming elixir in a drugstore glass, and then you'll open the door to your temple.

You will check stock, or sort vegetables, or read yesterday's mail. Soon you will squeeze a pair of shoes onto a customer, or you'll look for hat sizes, or you'll weigh turnips.

Running on a separate track all the time, your mind will be fishing, or wishing, or worrying. Likely it will be worrying—and of course about payday, for payday just won't reach. The note is overdue, the insurance has lapsed, the baby's teeth need attention, your wife seems too tired all the time, your job isn't much to begin with, and besides no one really appreciates you anyway.

Then, its *coffeetime*—sacred interval!—and you get a break. A little bit picked up in spirit, you come back to work and worry about the children's report cards, your daughter's dating habits or that she either did or will marry the wrong fellow too young, last month's bills, the neighbor's fence line, maybe you ought to see the doctor about yourself, yet, "Here I've worked twenty years and have no savings at all except that little bit of lapsed insurance"—and you're glad you've got it and wish the premiums were paid.

And then *lunchtime*—blessed break! You swallow a bowl of soup, bolt a sandwich, wonder why you are

nervous; some drugstore radio blares the word of one
great general's important word against another great
general's important word—you wish you knew which
set of stars on which shoulder had all the right of it and
in the back of your mind feel a little guilty because you
are not more concerned. But the whole business drops
through the grating of your mind out of sight, for you
must go by and make a payment on that small loan
overdue—and to do it you borrow from another small
loan outfit until payday.

Late getting back, you have seventeen customers—
sell three—and the boredom is unbearable along with the
wave of heat coming in from the already hot street. You
wish you had it as easy as your brother—who is getting
rich teaching school—or your sister—who married oil or
cattle—and after a while, eternity, it is *quittingtime*—
hallowed rest! But you know the boss knows that you
know the boss knows how poor a day you really had.
You get into five o'clock traffic, and if lucky you get
home at last, fighting all the way.

Even there the kids are cross, not cleaned up, your
wife exhausted, the landlord won't paint your house
though you've bought it four times in rent, your little
old garden is half-dead—in spite of your seven-dollar
water bill—so there's nothing to do but eat too much
supper since you haven't eaten right all day, and then,
loggy and tired and bored, you fall into bed at last,
muttering:

15

"Nothing that I did today matters!
 If I had put a label on everything I did today,
  it would have to read:
    This Product
    Is Not Guaranteed
    Beyond Sixty Days.
 It wasn't put together right;
  It wasn't made of the right stuff;
   It won't stand up under use;
    It will break down.
If I hadn't done a thing all day,
  it wouldn't matter!
Nothing I do matters
  or counts,
    or lasts after payday."

II

This man is Legion. There are thousands of him. And he is sick. Dangerously sick. He needs a spirit within that will give life real meaning. He needs something to take him over the dullness and the prosaicness of all his everydayness. This fellow is sick. He needs to be able to feel he has made some progress. He needs a feeling of significance. He needs to know that he matters. In some way he must get what he so desperately lacks—confidence, courage, faith, love of himself, and time. He needs to know that his part matters, that his life can be a contribution, that his yearnings can be met. He needs something bigger than he to consume him and set him on fire.

But his name is Legion—he is everywhere and his troubles are everywhere.

Yet he is still sick. The fact that most of us have whatever he has does not make us well. People like this are spiritually sick. All cities today have within them great lines of purposeless people—"deracinated hordes" whose only real desires are to be well fed, reasonably unbored, and fairly well clothed.

Occasionally one of them wakes up to the fact of his need. He begins to realize that although he does a number of things regularly and well, that although he thinks a number of thoughts, knows a reasonable number of facts, he suddenly has become quite sure that none of them are really worth thinking, doing, or knowing.

But how can he escape the pattern? How can he become what he is not? How can he get out of what drudgery and the everydayness of every day will do to him? How will he escape the consequences of his neglected salvation?

Nothing he does endures after payday.

Nothing he thinks has consequence.

Nothing he says matters.

All he sees decays.

All he loves dies.

All he wants disappears.

All he has dreamed collapses.

17

How can he escape unless he finds some things that endure? What will he do unless he finds something that has survival value beyond the first of the month?

Does anything endure? Is there a thing that will remain? How can he, surrounded by decay, find eternity, for what he is and loves? Every man ought to have some things that remain.

I watched a friend of mine offer to buy a handsome gun from the veteran craftsman who had made it. He was able to pay; he was interested enough to pay—and well.

The gun was a marvel of the builder's art. Many a day had gone into the inletting and chequering of that perfect walnut, the reshaped bolt and polished receiver, the true barrel and keen scope sight, the fine trigger assembly and honed action.

"I'll buy," said my friend. "How much?"

And the old man who had made it for himself, pouring years of skill and enjoyed work into the one perfect creation of his art, cradled the beautiful rifle across his arm, looked down at it, and said, "I made it for my own; nobody could buy it; there isn't *anything* that would *buy* it. Perhaps my son will want it."

My friend with me smiled and got a good lift from it as he said to me a little wistfully, "Every man ought to have something somewhere that he wouldn't sell for *anything*." *And that is true*. Every man ought to have right in the middle of his life something that he wouldn't sell for *anything*.

It ought to be there—something that endures, the thing, the one thing, that remains—right in the middle of his power, right in the middle of his life, right in the middle of where he has to live day by day—something that nothing can *buy*. Not for sale.

But what lasts? Nothing you can see lasts. Nothing tangible has eternal value. Houses cannot stay homes— stocks and bonds are not eternal—rifles rust—partnerships die—businesses fail—governments leave the gold standard —granite wears away.

Nothing you can see lasts. All tangibles perish; only intangibles survive. Time gets everything, and men are caught.

Does nothing endure? Is there that that remains, and can a man get it for himself, and for his fellows?

That is the goal of religion. It is religion—and it is always of the spirit that anything survives.

It is here, right here, that religion has something to say. It is here, right here, that the Christian faith begins to cry, "*These things remain* for any man who will take them!" Here Christianity begins to say, "*There is an eternal process at work among us.*"

All tangibles perish—the intangibles survive. The inexorable laws of life destroy all that can die. But the same laws of life that destroy all that can die create the conflict—the situation—in which all that is fit to live demonstrates its fitness for life. That is why our bodies die.

19

There is an eternal process at work among us. The Christian lives. This he believes, and in believing comes to new life, comes to a relationship with the eternal, the intangible, that that endures.

But what does he believe? How can it be that belief can do it? And what is the object of his belief?

III

What Christian can say it for them all? The Christ of each man's heart is different from that of other hearts. No Christian can speak for all other Christians. Personal, infinitely personal, is that inner grasp; but this, I believe, remains: that God made Man—made Man in His own image, made Man as the crowning, finishing act of His preparatory creation. But it remains also that God did not finish creating when He made Man. That is to say, creation continues, is not yet complete, is far short of completion. It has, then, remained: God made Man in His own image, crowning act of His preparation, as His own *agent* in the completion of creation; and so equipped this Man—who works, and rides busses, and has indigestion, and fusses with his neighbors—so equipped this Man that he could provide himself with the tools he would need to finish God's creation. It remains, further, that Man cannot be God's agent unless he has *responsibility*, that is, the ability to meet a situation. Responsibility is the ability to decide and the ability to put the thing over. But if Man has responsibility, he must have not only the ability to succeed; he must have also the ability to fail, to lose out, to defeat the Purpose.

If my agent has no power to fail, he is not my agent. He is just a tool. If he has power only to succeed, he has no responsible part and is but tool, hammer, anonymous puppet. But Man is no puppet. Of this I am sure. He is able, responsible, integer, soul, person. It still remains that Man has free moral choice. He is responsible to God. He can build or destroy. He not only has power to rob himself, but he can rob God for whom he is agent in the business of completing creation.

It remains long that Man has robbed himself and God as God's agent. The man I described in the beginning has the sickness that results from such a robbery. And his name is Legion. Yet it is contrary to God's nature to fail. God will not use his creation power, by which He made us, to make failure. This means that God chooses for us to build, not destroy, to finish, not fail. Therefore *God has put at work an eternal power to make Man finish creation*. One name for that power is *time*. This power presses every individual. It works with every culture and nation. It operates in every civilization, and it has always the same pattern and order. You can find the operation of this pattern in the death of every empire. The death of every dying man and nation attests it. You may find it in all life and every life. It is there to make God's agent finish creation.

21

It remains and has always appeared like this:[1] *cross, suffering, cleansing, grace, new life;* or *crisis, passion, purging, release, eternal being;* or *conflict, ordeal, catharsis, charisma, resurrection.*

It remains that the twin wheels of the inexorable are always seen to be in terms of Cross—Suffering, Crisis—Ordeal, Conflict—Passion. These are the grinding wheels of the inexorable. And by the "inexorable" I mean that these are powers, forces, that are written into life with such basic meaning that neither prayer nor entreaty nor any other force can remove them. They are inescapably and universally there, right in life's middle.

These are the burning fires: Cross! Ordeal!

These are the eternal destroyers that are in this world by God's will to mash all that will mash, to crush all that will collapse, to burn out all that will burn, to purge out all that is false, to destroy in you everything that can die. The tangibles perish. The things that you see cannot endure, but everything that does last lasts through ordeal, every human institution that survives survives out of crisis, every human value goes on existing *after* the Cross that tests it. *Everything eternal comes out of a crucible.* Every true religious word represents something that the relentless wheels of Cross and Ordeal could not crush.

All that lasts in life, all that lasts of you, all that lasts

[1] P. A. Sorokin in *The Crisis of Our Age* sees this pattern: crisis—ordeal—catharsis—charisma—resurrection. They are all New Testament terms.

of your family, all that lasts of your way of life, government, creed, law, philosophy, and even personality, comes along this route: Cross, Suffering, Cleansing, Grace, New Life.

IV

Now, it remains, too, that the power that destroys the dross becomes the preserver of the worthy thing.

The eternal process that destroys is the same power that makes Man finish creation. But every term we have used: Cross—Crisis—Conflict; Ordeal—Suffering—Passion; Cleansing—Purging—Catharsis; Grace—Release—Charisma; Resurrection—Eternal Being—New Life, every term is emblazoned all through the New Testament, the life, death, and ascension of Jesus Christ, the heart, purpose, and meaning of the Christian gospel.

It is *all* there, and, it remains, Jesus Christ is the cosmic, universal demonstration in time of this eternal principle of *Cross—Suffering—Cleansing—Grace—New Life*. He came to give that process meaning for us all. That is why He is true. He is why that is true. He demonstrates that this is back of him and ahead for us. This is why He is so vital, so tremendously vital; for He came to show in His own body, so that we might grasp it, the process that leads to the eternal. This pattern is common to all life. It remains that in Him all of life's meaning hangs together at last and stands demonstrated.

In Him and only in Him can the pattern my life must

take become one I can understand. It remains that all history reveals the operation of that pattern of Cross— Resurrection of which He, Christ, is the *cosmic demonstration*.

It remains that He, Jesus Christ, is the "hero with a thousand faces" sought by countless men and nations who never knew His name. He remains the clue they sought to the meaning of Man's life of travail.

He remains as never before since this pattern appeared in my own experience. I believe Him! Redeemer, Saviour, Exemplar, Leader, Lord, Son of God, *sent by God to make all religions but the true impossible*. Sent by God to make it impossible, ultimately, for men who can think to believe anything but truth. Sent by God to demonstrate even that the great powers of the rational minds of this world exist only to help this inexorable Cross burn everything else away but truth. Sent by God to show me what it all means. It ever remains that in Him a man can take the road life forces him to take without being made a sick and perishing thing apart from his creative purpose. In Him this Cross—Suffering—Cleansing—Grace— New Life has its only chance to find me eternal.

Only in Him it remains so that a man's creative function will be fulfilled, a man's enduring destiny will be consummated, and his own personal powers will be found worthy of eternity. Christ is God's meaning and life's meaning. He is life's Hero and Saviour. He by my believing surrender, He, Jesus Christ, can be appropriated as my personal possession, as my contemporary companion.

So far in Man's wild journey it remains that only by the discovery and appropriation of His own Cross—Suffering—Cleansing—Grace—New Life—only in Him and His can any human being surmount the pressures of the inexorable that life imposes. Only in Him is a man worthy of the eternal. Apart from Him we are all sick. Apart from Him I am sickest of all.

These things remain? Better say this thing remains: *He, Christ, Son of God, demonstrates, in His own body for me to receive, the pattern life will make me take to failure, unless I am content for Him to handle it with me as He handled it in Himself.*

Only in Him is it true that "though my body be destroyed, yet shall I see. . . ."

Having Him to make life's meaning make sense makes us capable of doing mighty, enduring things. It makes of a home a place that lasts. It makes what a man feels for a woman endure across all the chasms that time can bring and all the changes it can produce. It makes a man's love for his children an abiding thing. It makes of his everyday job not a humdrum thing, but it becomes an outpost from which he helps finish creation. Christ gives life meaning.

V

Tomorrow morning his alarm clock will go off about three hours too early. Since 1902 it has been calling him to grumble, turn over, reach for it, shut it off, and go back to the same old thing.

But it's different for him. He has sixty thousand patient, plodding miles of prayer behind him back and forth from the same old job. He has walked twice around the globe with God to and from the same old job.

The screaming whistle, the throbbing hammers, the thundering drop-forges, will salute him like an organ as he enters his smoking and ancient cathedral.

The glaring furnaces, full of steel so hot it spits and is slick, will cast the flaring light of the Spirit over his daily altar. He will walk all day long from shears to furnaces to hammer line to drop-forge among the "sheep of his pasture," for he is not only "foreman," he has become shepherd of their souls—souls of men who agonize for their daily bread too.

Of their needs and troubles they will speak to him. A sick child—an overdue note—a bond defaulted—a kinsman in trouble. He will do their first aid, and listen to their grief, and pass a hat to pay for a funeral.

For they are men in the crucible too. And on his way home he'll pass the mission he served for twenty-five years before it could become a church, the homes of little boys he helped raise up to be deacons in it, and the home of one he prayed thirty years to lead to Christ. And Buster, and Jim, and Red, and Sim, and Walter, and Fred, and Bob, and all the rest are better because

they know him—and all the way home little children will
call out to "Mr. Leonard" as he passes.

I know, because I worked there too; and it was so
then—twenty years ago.

He has learned through drought and flood, fire and loss,
sacrifice and the everydayness of every day—he has
learned, my father knows:

      Everything eternal comes out of a crucible,
    so from his outpost
      he is helping God finish creation.

CHAPTER TWO

If you then suddenly found yourself waiting for death,
in a stinking hole, while
the One you called Lamb,
Redeemer,
Lion of the tribe,
did quiet miracles in a near-by valley
instead of taking
His throne

and saving you . . .
Wouldn't you call Him to His duty?
Wouldn't you remind Him of his function?
Wouldn't you call Him to your rescue?
Wouldn't you, too, send disciples unto Jesus saying,
Art Thou He? or,
Do we look for another,
some other,
any other?
Do Your job, Messiah.
Throw off your disguise.

John!—and the heart message rises clear
and sharp—John! Listen to me!
I-can-no-more-come-to-you-than-I-can-
come-down-from-my-own-cross.
In the wilderness I could not turn stones
to bread, John.
In your death, dear John, I cannot save you
any more than I can save Myself.
Not and be true to the Mission.

MUST WE LOOK FOR ANOTHER?

I

"Art thou the coming one, or must we be looking for an additional One?"

Whatever you say of this gospel, you cannot call it dull. Anywhere there is dullness in its presentation, it is the presenter who is dull. The Christian faith staggers the imagination. It is the most stirring drama that has ever excited man.[1]

At the same time the Christian religion is simple. Sublimely simple. It means one thing: *eternal life*. In the

[1] See Dorothy Sayers' stimulating *Creed or Chaos.*

midst of *time*. By the strength and under the eyes of God.[2]

And Christianity is the only religion with which we now have to deal. No other religion has longer the power to stir.[3]

But at the same time Christianity is no sacred stock pile of ethical and social purposes for the improvement or even the preservation of matters generally. Those who make the main issue out of what Christianity has done incidentally for Western civilization create a social gospel, emasculate the Redeemer's intention, and leave the gospel a witless and driveless social anomaly.

It is for Man—not for civilization—that the gospel is given. Wolfgang Goethe once wrote, "Mankind is always advancing, and man always remains the same." It is to Man that the gospel speaks: to Man who in the midst of all change and progress himself never changes.

And it speaks of Jesus Christ. No other. One of England's best [4] once said somewhere that "mankind cannot be too often reminded that there was once a man named Socrates." I suppose that is so, but it is infinitely more important to allow no man to lose the knowledge that One named Jesus once stood among us. "No one who has once absorbed a ray of Christ's light can ever again be

[2] See Adolf Harnack, *What Is Christianity?*
[3] See Kenneth Scott Latourette, *The Christian Outlook.*
[4] John Stuart Mill.

as though he had never heard of him." [5] For Christianity has a Founder who was Himself what He taught, and it is my concern and the concern of all pulpits to lead us to steep ourselves in Him. That is our chief business.

II

Is this He?

But who has ever understood Him? Men still find Jesus hard to grasp. Jewish scholars, sincere truth searchers, half-read experts in comparative religions, sophomore agnostics, once-born pilgrims, bewildered believers, still ask, *"Why Jesus Christ? Is this really He?"* And the general state of affairs in this "Christian" world leads some of those who have believed most fully to ask again, "Is this really He; must we not look for help in another direction too?"

Such questions came in the mind of one very close to Him. There is nothing before the Cross more poignantly touching than this question of the Baptist when he sent loyal men to ask what the prisoner of Herod could not ask in person: *"Art thou he that should come, or do we look for another?"* an additional one? one besides?

John's bewilderment is not hard to understand. For two centuries tragedy had piled on tragedy in his land. Since Antiochus, who said he was Savior twenty decades before, there had been no peace. The great kingdom of the

Maccabees, born in revolt, had blown up from its internal violence; and outsiders had gnawed the remains. The harsh Roman foot was upon everything. That pretender out of Edom, Herod, had hurt Israel in every joint.

As far as human sight could go, it looked as if Israel were beyond redemption. All the glorious old prophecies sounded like dreams—or lies. Despair ruled—of what possible use an earthly crown or any political possession? Prestige, wealth, effort, devotion—all were empty values.

The only possible hope was for a complete new kingdom—*Messiah*.

But in John's day even this hope was all mixed up.

The older prophets spoke, indeed, of a glorious future kingdom—God Himself would come down, destroy enemies, make justice, peace, and joy; then a wise and mighty king of David's house would appear. But now some of their interpreters were saying that they meant Israel would be Son of David.

Newer prophets had said Messiah's rule would be world wide and so would His judgment, for Diaspora had widened Jewry's horizon.

Other prophets were crying for moral purification. Now moral responsibility must be met—God must be holy to those of whom He would demand holiness.

Another stream of teaching held that only a remnant would know Messiah—open profaneness barred the masses; individual salvation was becoming a concern.

Others were saying: "Earth not a final goal"—"something new from heaven to earth"—"Transcending all earthly"—"He with God from the beginning"—"He will do by superhuman means." But the older people still, says Harnack, believed that God Himself would assume the scepter, destroying, founding, championing; and every man would sit under his own fig tree in his own vineyard, eating—with his foot on his enemy's neck. *When Messiah comes*. All this was in John's background.

If *you* had been told all your life that you were a child of promise, had been reared in an atmosphere of revolt, and revulsion, and longing; if *you* had found yourself a mission that would not let you go, had discovered that God now demanded justice and mercy instead of priestly and showy ceremonial; if *you* were convinced that help would come from God when men repented, had run to the precipice proclaiming, "Repent!" and thousands had heard and repented; if *you* carried a whole parcel of contradicting preachments about Messiah in your head, but *in spite of that* knew yourself to be His forerunner, and had sounded true and clear, and had seen heaven open and a dove descend and light upon Him, and if you had baptized Him and called Him Lamb of God; if *you* then suddenly found yourself waiting for death, in a stinking hole while the One you called Lamb, the King, the Priest-Prophet, Messiah, Sin Bearer, Redeemer, Lion of the tribe, did quiet miracles in a near-by valley instead of taking His throne and saving you, wouldn't you call Him to His duty? Wouldn't you remind Him of his function? Wouldn't you call Him to your rescue? Wouldn't you wonder at his distance from your need, his calmness, his indifference?

Wouldn't you, too, send disciples unto Jesus saying, "Art Thou He?" or, "Do we look for another, some other, *any other?*"

Do Your job, Messiah. Throw off Your disguise.

If there is nothing before the Cross more poignant than John's question, there is nothing more edifying than our Lord's answer:

And in that same hour he cured many; . . . and . . . answering said, . . . Go your way, and tell John what things ye have seen and heard; how that the blind see, the lame walk, the lepers are cleansed, the deaf hear, the dead are raised, to the poor the gospel is preached. And blessed is he, whosoever shall not be offended in me.

This is He!

III

Jesus sent a simple answer—pregnant with meaning. For centuries men have known of the love of Jesus for John the Baptist. Jesus sent him a warm and simple answer.

But, for that matter, this sufficient Christ brought the whole world a gospel which is much simpler than most

34

churches and all theologians will allow it to be. His gospel is a simple gospel—and for that very reason more stern and more universally applicable. A man cannot evade this sufficient Christ of the simple gospel on the subterfuge of a misunderstood Christology.

Jesus promised that *eternal life would cut through time by God's grace and mercy*, but He also said it is God *or* mammon, eternal *or* earthly, soul *or* body, humility *or* self, love *or* selfishness, truth *or* lie. A man has to make up his mind. It is God and the eternal for him, or it is the world and time.

The gospel as Jesus proclaimed it had always to do with the Father. He leads men to God not alone by what He says, John, but still more by what He does, and most by who He is, and ultimately *by what He suffers.*

"Come unto Me!" He cries, and when under the travail of His mission men begin to see that it is by Him that blind, leprous, possessed, and deaf are cured, when they see and note those to whom the gospel is preached, then will there dawn the New Vision—vision of the glory with which the Father has entrusted Him.

He *is* the way to the Father—"not as mere factor is He connected with the gospel." He *is* its personal realization and its strength. This He will remain.

But if this gospel points always to the Father,[6] what do

[6] In taking advantage of the insights of the great Harnack I have tried never to minimize the Person of Jesus by exclusion in favor of the Father, whom Harnack seems to make altogether central.

you want with your Christ? He brought nothing new,
they say.

I answer with Wellhausen and Harnack. It is quite true
that what Jesus expressed, what John the Baptist had proclaimed before Him, this repentance-gospel, was also in
the prophets; and traces can be found even in the Jewry
of the time. Without their knowledge the Pharisees had it.

But, unfortunately, they had a lot else. With them it
was all weighted, darkened, distorted, rendered ineffective, and deprived of its force by a thousand things they
held to be religious and as important as mercy and
judgment.

They reduced everything to one dead level. They had
choked the long-opened spring of holiness with sand and
dirt. They had diverted its waters with the silt from a
thousand petty laws, rubbish the priests and theologians
had dreamed up.

Now, *what was new?*

The spring of holiness had burst forth afresh and had
broken a new way for itself through the rubbish.

What was new? *Purity* was new. And after two thousand years purity is *still* new. Purity was new—and the
Personality was new.

Mere words are nothing—they all had the words, but
here was the *Personality of Purity* who could show men
the Father, and that was *brand-new.*

And He saw John, and heard John, and recognized

the forerunner, and accepted John's repentance-message and preached it Himself—and on the lips of Jesus, John's terrible message became a message of love and joy.

The Spirit of the Lord is upon me, because He hath anointed me to preach the gospel. . . .
Come unto me, all ye that labor and are heavy laden, and I will give you rest. Take my yoke upon you, and learn of me; and ye shall find rest unto your souls. For my yoke is easy, and my burden is light.

They knew God as Tyrant, cursing any omission of ceremonial law in His house. He—this new person—breathed in God's presence.

They could find God only in what they called His law and had dug it into a labyrinth—a prairie-dog warren of dark passages, closed alleyways, secret entrances. He—this new person—saw and felt Him everywhere and called Him Father.

They had option on the meaning of a thousand of His commandments and assumed they had title to Him as well. He—the new one—knew only one commandment.

They had shaped their religion into an earthly trade—detestable!

He—this new one—was living what had happened to Him, proclaiming a living Father, and my soul's nobility.

What was new? *Purity* was new, and *Personality* was new, and the *Proclamation*, the simple proclamation:

37

mourning and laughing,
weeping and dancing,
wealth and poverty,
plenty and thirst,
health and illness,
children's games and politics,
sowing and reaping,
leaving home and homesickness,
weddings and burials,
rich houses and graves,
barren lands and rich farms,
the lord of the vineyard and vines,
pearl merchants and idle laborers,
shepherds and lost sheep,
fishermen with fish,
women with lost coins and dead sons,
issues of blood and empty pocketbooks,
bread of heaven and water in a well,
food that spoils, stones and serpents,
ravens and ripe grain, colts and children,
lilies, sparrows, roof tops,
regal glory and a prostitute's tears,
the tyrant's power lust and a child's innocence,
five loaves and two fishes.

In all this everyday simplicity He strikes the mightiest notes; He cuts an inexorable alternative; *He leaves us no escape.*

38

This is He!
and He says, in effect, "Go and show John once more that *Saving Activity* in the form of Pure Personality is here."

"By my vanquishing misery, need, disease, John, my people, the poor—those who wait for the consolation of Israel—can see a new day.

"This *Saving Activity*, John, is the *seal of the Mission*. Be strong, dear John! God is at work among His people, the poor—those who have waited for Him. To them, John, is the message beamed."

To these here who have waited is this hope sent, and to them, before all, is the forgiveness of sin directed which makes possible the Kingdom.

You see, fire is kindled by fire. Personal life can respond best to personal forces. Let us rid ourselves of our dogmatic sophistries that seek to corner Christ for some little kingdom of our own.

God is master of His own mercies. He will show mercy where He will.

But history, two thousand years of it, says that it is Jesus, in His mission to men, who brings the weary and the heavy-laden to the Father.

This, in part, is the message Jesus sent with His heart across the miles to the beloved Baptist. And then He thought of His own time of imprisonment and Cross. *As He thought of John's grave He remembered His own* and called the messengers back for a postscript.

"Tell John," He whispers it. "Tell John, happy is that one who doesn't stumble over me."

Thinking of Cross and Death because of the thought of John's bloody grave, His heart sends a deeper word: "John, dear John, you wonder at My method; you wonder why I leave you there. John!"—and the heart message rises clear and sharp—"John! Listen to Me!

"I can no more come to you than I can come down from My own cross.

"In the wilderness I could not turn stones to bread, John. In your death, dear John, I cannot save you any more than I can save Myself. *Not and be true to the Mission.*

"Don't stumble over this, John. It's different from what you wanted—but so is My Cross. It will be a 'scandal' to many, and they shall stumble."

And stumble they did, and so did I. And you?

IV

But that grave at which we stumble—it brings another postscript which really is the message of Jesus. It says, in Dorothy Sayers' thrilling words: "For whatever reason God chose to make man as he is—limited and suffering and subject to sorrows and death—He had the honesty and the courage to take His own medicine." [7]

Whatever His purpose for creation and for me, He

[7] Sayers, *op. cit.*, p. 2.

has played the same game and by the same rules. For Jesus, son of Joseph, carpenter from Nazareth, was "in fact and in truth Son of God in the most literal sense."

It was His grave that the Father opened to complete this gospel, and

"This grave was the birthplace of the indestructible belief that death is vanquished, that there is a life eternal."

It is useless to cite Plato or to point to the Persian religion (or to Egypt) or the literature of later Judaism. All that is sunk, perished.

But the certainty of the Resurrection and life eternal which is bound up with the grave in Joseph's garden lives. And upon the conviction that Jesus *lives* we still base all our hopes of citizenship in an Eternal City.

He delivered them "who through fear of death were all their lifetime subject to bondage."

Wherever death is terrorless, wherever present pain is balanced with a future hope of glory, wherever life and self are conquered, it is bound up with the conviction that Jesus Christ has passed through death. That God. . . .

Ours is a strange new world—of progress and retrogression, of emancipation and slavery. Mankind climbs and slips onto a high plateau loaded with his new gadgets, concepts, and philosophies.

It is a new age—an age of progress—for common men, we were told once, and believed it.[8]

In this day, fraught with possibilities, the man of any feeling will gratefully receive the added hours given each day by technology and the added years given by medical science. He will be pleased with the added conveniences that science can devise and the boons of pleasure that freedom from slavish toil can save for him. He will take most gratefully all the tokens the development of mankind will bring him.

But inside—where he lives alone—he knows very well that his situation inwardly is unchanged. As Goethe said in the beginning, Mankind is always advancing, but man is always the same. The problems that agitate his own guilt, his own soul, these are not altered by progress—not at all.

He still has to have this sufficient Jesus.

Must we look for another?

In the midyears of his great powers, lecturing extempore to classes of six hundred from all schools of the University of Berlin, Harnack said, and a student took it down:

Gentlemen, when a man grows older, . . . he does not find, if he possesses any inner world at all, that he is advanced by the external march of things, by the "progress of civilization." Nay, he finds himself, rather, where he was

[8] But see John Baillie, *The Belief in Progress.*

42

before, and forced to seek the sources of strength which his forefathers also sought.

He is forced to make himself a native of the kingdom of God, the kingdom of the Eternal, the kingdom of Love; and he comes to understand that it was only of this kingdom that Jesus Christ desired to speak . . . and he is grateful to Him for it.[9]

This is he. There is no other. Let us break bread together on our knees—Let us drink wine together on our knees—Let us praise God together on our knees.

[9] Unknown to Harnack, these lectures were taken down in shorthand by a German student. Later published as *What Is Christianity?* they were translated into English by T. Bailey Saunders. This message is barely mine. It amounts to a digest of certain portions of Harnack's little book and is intended to be recognized as such.

CHAPTER THREE

O Lamb of God, my need is great, indeed!
My need is o'er pressing and urgent!

I need Thy redemption—
   not alone from my shallow concepts and
         these *careless* hands,
   not alone from what my *hasty* feet
and *slippery tongue* do to me and to men,
   not alone from this *selfish heart*.

I need redemption from me—to be redeemed
         from myself,
         and from what I
always make of myself, and from the unsavory
brew I always cook up when left alone in the
         kitchen.

I NEED THAT LAMB

JOHN THE BAPTIST WAS NO ACCIDENT. HE DIDN'T JUST
happen. John the Baptist was one of those strange flaming
meteors that occasionally flare for short terms across the
sky of human personality.

He blazed his way into a grave that no one knows.
He was never quiet. He stood with his courage in his
teeth, facing a crowd of the "best" men Judaism could
make, to say, "God does not have to have you. Do not
take it to yourselves that you are children of Abraham.
If God wants children of Abraham, he can fertilize
these stones to get them."

He was God's finger pointing a new path—the path all little lambs could tread—but the greatest thing he ever did, or said, or thought, came the day he stood at the edge of his waiting congregation and said: "Behold the Lamb of God, that taketh away the sin of the world." [1]

I

A highly trained European theologian once passed on a deeply appreciated observation. "Your theology," he said, and kindly, "is deficient in its grasp of sin; consequently, your concept of salvation is a shallow thing."

He spoke of American theology in general and the thought of my own group in particular. I took it to myself for us all. What if it is true?

What if we have made sin more act than attitude, more flesh than spirit, more general than particular, more national than personal?

What if in baptizing our millions we have failed to show them the enemy?

What if we have missed the biblical meaning in spite of our laborious exegeses?

What if in our glib diagnostic diatribes we have glossed over sin's real habitat, sin's true nature, sin's universal effect, and sin's eternal origin?

What if our refusal to understand sin has become a

[1] See Lee R. Scarborough, *How Jesus Won Men.*

boomerang to beat us about the shoulders already bowed under an institutional burden, made up of our cargo of thousands of unredeemed on our rolls?

Are we producing a race of people "saved" from sins they never wanted to commit—"innocens socordens," as Tactius says, "harmless (good) through stupidity"?

In a prayer meeting of some Norwegian Baptists a woman began to rejoice aloud—so a friend tells me. "Thank God," she cried, "I'm saved! Saved from tobacco, saved from drink, saved from the theater!" And the people rejoiced with her.

Next day her pastor went around to follow up the "conversion." "I did not know you smoked," he said. "I'm so glad at your release."

"Oh, I never smoked in my life," was the calm reply.

The pastor, startled, pressed on his way: "But you have at last been freed from the terrible drink habit, and we rejoice." Indignantly she cried, "Never, Sir, has a drop of such passed my lips!"

Disconcerted now the pastor groped his way to her obvious sin. "Then let us thank God," he said, "that at last the temptations of the theater no longer hold you."

"But, Pastor," she disclaimed, "I was never in one in my life!"

"Saved!"—from sins she never wanted to commit.

The pastor left, conscious that she had not been freed and now likely never would be freed from that attitude of sin that made her the worst gossip in his parish.

Saved! It sounds as if she had got hold of a fragment of a kind of American theology.

You can't get such an idea of sin from Isaiah, or Jesus, or Paul, or Luther. Sin is something worse than act. It is that fearful something that fathers all sinful acts. Somehow it is source, root, and tree—before it is blossom, flower, or fruit. It is inner, personal, real, universal. It is a "perpetual moral obliquity." It is an ever-present set to the soul. It is incontrovertibly impinged on the id, the ego, the self—defying castigation, incantation, exorcism, and reformation.

The *self* feeds it, sends it out, then receives it back multiplied. The *self* exudes it, then breathes it in. It cannot be fully confessed, nor can it be denied. It lives there. As long as Self is Self and I am I. It expresses itself in my self-love and in my refusal to love myself. It is my darkness, my old Man of the Mountain who rides Sinbad till death. He defies me; he multiplies himself out of my strength. From him come all my anxiety and care which are but prelude to overt sin,[2] all my self-pity and jealousy, all my prejudices and preoccupations, all my narrowness and bigotry. Self!—Self!—Self! The source of all Man's glory is the breeding place of all his woe. He sits there, proudly, defiantly, sucking the juices from my soul, as Isaiah says, atrophying—attacking my soul's ability to see its own sin.

[2] See Sören Kierkegaard, *The Concept of Dread* and *The Sickness unto Death*.

When men persist in sin, they lose the power of knowing sin is there; they lose their ability to hear and understand eternal things. Little by little we lose possession of the very faculties by which we might be saved.

All history says it is so. Persia finally committed the fatal sin of refusing to see herself as she was—and died. So, Greece, Egypt, Carthage, the Holy Roman Empire, and the German. And the British? And the American?

All stories have had the same ending. No empire has ever dealt with its own sin. All apparently lose the very faculties by which redemption could come as they proceed further and further into their willfulness.

And as with nations, so with men. All must always have a god. When the true God is unknown or refused, mankind will have him some other god to direct him.[3]

Most likely that new god is one he has made himself. The tragedy of human nature is somehow wrapped up in the business of making these lesser gods.

The final tragedy comes when Man deifies himself—when he cries, "Thou art my god, O Myself!" But always when he makes himself God, he makes himself Devil.

O Lamb of God, my need is great, indeed! My need for redemption is o'er pressing and urgent!

I need Thy redemption—not alone from my shallow concepts and careless hands, not alone from what my

---

[3] "Man has always some God or an idol," said Luther.

hasty feet and slippery tongue do to me and to men, not alone from this selfish heart; I need redemption from *me*. My need for redemption is to be redeemed from myself. To be redeemed from what I make of myself—for when I manufacture myself, the product is inevitably rejected. I make myself inevitably less than I ought to be—eternally and infallibly an unholy mess.

I need redemption, like my nation needs redemption, from the unsavory brew I always cook up when left alone in the kitchen. The blight of the world—the sin that is myself and yourself. The world blight that John was facing—that we face together now—a deadly damning blight.

II

But the world has long had a dream about that blight. All the pages of the history of searching Man give evidence of Man's great dream. Even those pages written on stone with crude brushes dipped in ancient dye give mute word of a shared dream.

Man has dreamed that some day—somehow—his limiting ineffectiveness, his finite failure, his eternally present sinfulness, could be taken away. Man has always dreamed that the unholiness he has concocted might be cleaned up. He dreams it about his nation, his family, and with a most personal application about himself.

Somehow, somewhere, sometime there will come one holy enough, and fine enough, and unselfish enough to lead man out of what he has always made of himself.

Dostoevsky's Father Zossima understood that for the Russian peasant "it was the most important thing in the world to find Someone before whom he could fall down and worship." And Father Zossima understood, too, that great peasant dream that *"one day He will come to us, too, and rule over all the earth, according to the promise."*

Charlie Knight, returning to Ogbomosho from his first hunt for African buffalo, stopped to tell an aged chieftain just whom he had come to Nigeria to represent. After he had finished his word of the Nazarene, the old man said in his heathen Yoruba, *"Aye, I know of Him; I have heard His voice in the treetops at night."*

Eugene Hill, refugeeing some years ago ahead of the advancing Japanese armies, in a little village, heard the reply in provincial Chinese of an old woman to his word about that One: *"I have always felt there was such a One, but no one could tell me His name."*

The dream is everywhere—and the hope. Through all the centuries man has lived in hope—the last emotion that leaves before sanity goes. Dostoevsky, condemned to death, lined up with his companions for execution, waiting for the word that would blast out their lives, heard the galloping horse that carried the pardon of the czar. But some of his companions never knew they had been released—hope had already died, and they were insane.

However near insanity the race of Man now seems,

still Man has not lost the hope. And his dream still is that somewhere there is Someone who can make things right. In this hope he dreams of pardon, of forgiveness, of release, of having power to defeat sin.

On the flyleaf of that fine novel *Green Dolphin Street,* there appears a quotation from Evelyn Underhill that points out the three great desires of man's dreaming:

The *first* makes him a wanderer over the earth, for he longs for a Holy City, El Dorado, Zion.

The *second* makes him a searching lover, for he craves someone to understand him.

The *third* makes him a saint, for he has a holy desire to become clean and free of himself.

Because of Man's dream anyone who could build a city, or evince a modicum of understanding, or do a cleansing service could get a following. Anyone who showed any of the traits of Messiah could lead a long procession.

See those thousands of Crusaders following the poor bald mule of Peter the Hermit—a mule made bald by their clutching at his hair for the sake of his spiritual power. See those other thousands seeking the same Holy Land behind the aimless wanderings of a silly goose pointed out by an addled priest as God's leader for Crusade.

How old is the searching! How ancient is the dream! How poignant is the hope!

The world has wept and prayed for deliverance from itself, Israel in Egypt, Israel under Moses, Israel in

Babylon. *O Jerusalem, how forget thee! And the hope!*

Under Ezra they began to say again, "Some day, surely, Someone will come!" And as the Greek language came in, they coined a name for Him—a translation into Greek of the Old Testament yearnings—"O Erchomenos," "The-One-Who-Will-Come," they called Him.

In Persia men were looking for the Son of Light. In Greece they searched for Logos, the Divine Word. In Rome they were looking for any ritual, or any blood bath, or any power that would release them from their own sense of wrong.

The old circle stones that still show on some of the ancient slopes of England were seats where men met to find out how they might continue in spite of the flesh.

And in pagan Germany when there were still upwards of fifty tribes of the Germans wandering wild over the face of the earth, their huge white bodies bloated after the long winter spent lying around in little huts, drinking mead and eating while their women did the work, even those lazy warriors were looking for anything that meant freedom (*vrai-doom*). The priests of Charlemagne baptized four thousand of them from one tribe on the Weber early in the ninth century.

And today? Except for the first Christian century I am convinced that not since the sixth century B.C. in India, when Gautama arose, has there been such a widespread consciousness of lostness, aimlessness, emptiness, and frustration.

And the dream? It appears as what Luccock calls *"a hunger for affirmation"* in our poetry, drama, novels, movies, self-help literature, and even in the comics— Superman and Supermouse. The dream still lives.

John knew He would come, and he preached it. *"There cometh One. . . ."*

Back to his wilderness hut he went at night, to fall down beside his pallet and cry, *"O Lord, I did not misunderstand!* There is an impression in my soul that will not die. It cannot die. Oh, when will He come? O Lord, let me see Thy Lamb Whose stripes will free us from ourselves!"

Repent! Repent! There comes One. *O my soul! Cling always to this hope and surety.*

Repent! Repent! Lo, He cometh!
> *Come, O Holy Dove, point out to my seeking heart the face of the One God has sent.*

Repent ye! Thy King cometh unto thee.
> *O Holy Dove! when wilt thou light on Him who is to redeem us from ourselves?*

III

And He came. Flatly, emotionlessly, the Scripture tells of the Great Event.

In the one line the undersong is "Oh, when will He come?" And then in the next . . . ? "On the morrow [John] seeth Jesus coming unto him, and saith, [not even "cried"] Behold [how long the wait for that word!] the

Lamb of God, that taketh away the sin of the world!"
A dream come true!

The minor prophets, from whom John is supposed
to have grasped his picture of Messiah's function, do not
know Him as Lamb. They speak of Shepherd, Lion,
Ruler, King, but not of Lamb. It is Isaiah who knew
Him as a "sheep that before its shearer is dumb." It is
Isaiah, and Genesis, Exodus, and Leviticus that speak of
lambs and sacrifices and offerings. It was to Abraham
that God promised a lamb for a burnt offering.

In spite of John's later query about the functions of
the Messiah, in spite of the agitated message he sent from
prison to remind Jesus of His function as Axman, Leader,
I have no choice but to feel that John got his idea of
Messiah-Lamb from the passage that calls Him Lamb.

He knew Old Testament scripture; he was familiar
with the sacrificial signifiance of lambs—the law of the
sacrifice, that a lamb must be without blemish before it
could carry sin away.

Surely Isaiah's immortal section on the Lamb was a
part of his very soul *whether he understood it or not.*

John knew this Lamb—

"As a lamb that is led to the slaughter,
    and as a sheep that before its shearers is dumb,"
oppressed but silent.

John had yet to learn it in his own body. *But every
time a thing that is good suffers, it releases its redemption to the need around it.* That is why good men must

55

be silent about their suffering. It is why the Lamb would
be silent.

There is *always* in redemption some of *tragedy* and
suffering. Berdyaev and Dostoevsky, the Russians,
grasped it. How poignantly humorous that we would
try to take the tragedy out of the Christian religion!
You can't take it out of life, and you can't take it out of
the religion of life. It is written into life.

John could not see it, but Christ had to be despised
and rejected, a man of sorrows, not unacquainted with
grief. How could he have come as a Prince of the Realm
if He came to understand man's devils, gutters, and his
sin? He *had* to know grief in order to understand. He *had*
to be tragedy bearer to be sin bearer. It is written in.
He *had* to die, and not easily. How could one master life
without conquering death?

John had not been preaching a reform of the old. He
was proclaiming the arrival of the new. And the prerequi-
site for its reception is still repentance.

"All we like sheep have gone astray"; we have turned
every one to the path he has picked out for himself. But
the Lord is gracious,

"And . . . hath made to light on him the iniquity of
us all," in order that God's dream of us might be true.
The Deliverer—behold Him!

In *Redemption and Revelation*, H. Wheeler Robinson
tells of a French skeptic who wandered into a Paris cathe-

dral during the singing of that twenty-third portion of
the Mass which begins,

"Agnus Dei, qui tollis peccata mundi,
misere nobis."

(*"Lamb of God, who taketh away the sin of the
world, be merciful to us."*)

Pierced by its beauty, the skeptic cried, "Lamb of God!
If only he could! What a dream!"

The gospel says, He can! and, He has! And that
means *forgiveness* for us, *suffering* for Him.

IV

But you will permit a word about that forgiveness?
If we have not grasped the true nature of sin, we have
missed forgiveness too.

There is no forgiveness on earth or in heaven that can
reach my heart except as I adopt the Lamb's own suffering pattern of the Cross and forgive. It is my forgiveness
that must release God's forgiveness. I cannot receive
from Him and deny to you. I am forgiven as I forgive,
which makes my selfish heart suffer and shatters its sin.
In the light of the Cross, in the prayer of the Lamb, I,
forgiving, receive forgiveness.

And another word? There is no forgiveness in heaven,
or beyond heaven, that can remove what sin has done.
God's forgiveness never uncooks a brain already cooked
in alcohol; God's forgiveness does not destroy the
scars—they remain.

57

Forgiveness happens only between concerned personalities. God and me; you and me. It cannot clear up the debris. It cannot restore a home smashed beyond the power of personality to restore; it cannot give grown children the father they needed when they were little.

Even though that old man whom I buried made a profession of his faith and trusted Christ for forgiveness, there still was no profession of faith possible to him that would see wiped out the decades of hell he had strewn over the earth and in the hearts of his children who could not forget, even at the funeral.

Not even God's forgiveness can fix that home as it should have been fifty years before.

Forgiveness just picks a man up where he is, puts him back together, then wipes out the horror of the past with the light of the future that it releases in him. The scars stay, but He gives grace to live with scars even though scar tissue can cause pain.

If forgiveness can happen only between personalities, it is because personality only can effect redemption.

Only divine Person can effect divine redemption—so the Lamb came to demonstrate that suffering releases redemption; to empty death of its horrors forever; to restore what could be restored only by forgiveness; to secure for God all that sin left salvageable, to redeem me from me, and from what I would become if left to myself.

But the thing we have never been able to forgive God, we humans, is that He made His Lamb to be a *suffering* Lamb.

In our minds, whether we will permit its expression or not, is buried in some form the feeling that

He didn't have to *do that to Him*—speaking of Cross.

We do not seriously object to His being poor; we will even forgive His refusal to defend Himself with the host of His Father's servants. But Man has never forgiven Him:

His refusal to turn stones to bread,

His acceptance of the Cross-way.

Two things are repugnant to us—they remain so in our half-redeemed state: the *duty*, the *work*, that binds us here on earth and the *cross*, the *suffering*, through which life must go. This feeling is the last word of Man's presumptuous, colossally ridiculous accusation. It is our last chance to pin responsibility for this evil world on someone other than ourselves.

We have blamed Satan, the Adversary, demons, knowledge (*scientia*); ignorance, insanity, animal nature; but most of all *we try to blame God*, and the sin is Luciferrian.

Never! Never yet has Mankind reconciled himself to his own responsibility. God made Him Lamb. *We* made Him *suffering* Lamb.

We had made Him suffering Lamb from the beginning. The blight determined the suffering.

We have yet to learn God's *use* of the suffering we made unavoidable for Him and for us.

Blessed be the great God who can use the suffering He would not deny His own Son in order that in His own body He could demonstrate the lostness of being fully Man and the savedness of being fully God.

How gracious of God to use the suffering clay to make the healing balm!

All suffering men ought to learn that. The suffering man who gave that immortal drama *The Green Pastures* caught it. Do you recall the very last scene?

Gabriel finds "de Lawd" sitting in a deep study, midstage. At last the time has come to blow. Gabriel reaches for his long brass horn which hangs down his neck. He rubs the mouthpiece lovingly; he steps to the window puffing his black cheeks in delighted anticipation—so long he has wanted to blow his horn and wind up this pointless earth drama.

"Lawd, is de time come for me to blow?"

"Not yet, Gabriel. I'm just thinkin'."

"What about, Lawd?" (And the soft singing of the choir stops as they listen too.)

" 'Bout somethin' de boy tol' me. Somethin' 'bout Hosea, and himself. How dey foun' somethin'."

"What, Lawd?"

"Mercy. Through *sufferin'*, he said."

"Yes, Lawd."

"I'm tryin' to find it, too. It's awful impo'tant. It's

awful impo-tant to all de people on my earth. Did he mean dat even God must suffer?"

Then (those who have seen it and heard it will never forget) the little girl's voice, 'way off stage in the distance (a master stroke, for who could have portrayed it on stage?)—the thin, high voice of a little Negro girl: "Oh, look at him! Oh, look, dey goin' to make him carry it up dat high hill! Dey goin' to nail him to it! Oh, dat's a terrible burden for one man to carry!"

God stands and murmurs "Yes" in acceptance (of the pattern of suffering Man has made necessary?). The heavenly beings, seeing Him smile, draw back, relieved. And the whole chorus bursts into

"Hallelujah! King Jesus!"

God still smiles; the lights fade; the singing becomes fortissimo.[1]

> Behold the Lamb!
> The suffering Lamb—
> who carries sin away.

[1] From *The Green Pastures*, copyright 1930 by Marc Connelly, and reprinted by permission of Rinehart & Co., Inc., Publishers.

61

. . . long rows of thick-jawed, overstuffed, inventory-
worried, high-blood-pressured, cardiac, successful young
men

      mingling with
     their blood brothers,
      and no others,

    over half-baked ham,
    watery green beans,
     sick apple slaw,
     and soggy pie,

listening to
 anemic platitudes
  mouthed after dinner
   by some pale prelate
 who salts his sop
    with
  slang and stale jokes

      to hold their "interested,"
       bored eyes.

Then "all join hands and *really* sing"—

Sweet fellowship, stirring beyond words!
 But isn't all this a far cry from that piercingly
  personal death warrant:
 *"For God so loved the world that he gave
     his only begotten Son"?*

THE DAYSPRING

I

Up where the foothills of the colorado begin to level out I stopped with a visitor to our country at a beautiful spring—source of supply for a valiant little creek that sets out to drain all the hills it can.

My friend and I wanted desperately to drink. A rider far down the range had pointed to the spring as the only one around. But when we knelt to drink, the spring was so clogged with dead matter that we drew back with distaste. The once beautifully clean source was all cluttered up!

The source of our light is spoken of as a "spring,"

spring of the day—the place where the dawn begins, synonym for dawn within the heart of God, the figure of the beginning of God's love for all the races. Paul has it in mind in the introductory phrases of his grand theological work. Paraphrased it could read, *"For in the gospel the dawn comes up for us in terms of God's righteousness given from faith to faith, for the just live from faith."*

This is the Dayspring. This is the welling up of our dawn; where God's righteousness eternally begins its work with us is always in the realm of faith—ours and His. But the source is eternally being cluttered and covered over. Men go on forgetting that God always begins His work in terms of their lostness—He never begins anywhere else—and He always begins in terms of faith. That faith of which repentance and belief are component parts.

At times we have almost lost the Dayspring. Men crowd into the waters of Christianity down below the source. They make what Christianity has done incidentally to be the main thing, the source, and forget that *the New Testament has no word for any man who remains an unbeliever.* Not a single word except: *Repent and believe the gospel.* This is the beginning of your faith.

The New Testament code of conduct has no claim upon any unbeliever. It is not for you. The only message of the New Testament for men outside the grace of God is: *Repent and believe the gospel.*

This God of the New Testament, this God who presses His claim to all lost men, this God in whom the Source takes its source, is never a reformer, setting out to revise by legislation; never a social worker, coming in to look over a "case"; never a program planner, saving the world with bureaus. He is not a slogan maker, nor a banner waver at the conventions of do-gooders; nor an arbitrator, hoping by the peace of the two to make peace for the many; nor is He a self-improvement expert, giving men a little formula to recite before their mirrors every morning.

He *never* was, as some have felt, the manager of a guide service for metaphysically-minded tourists, who are wandering around on leisurely jaunts; nor has He ever been a sort of glorified housing authority, also expert in juvenile and senile delinquency, passing out relief.

The New Testament knows practically nothing of social needs. This God has not even a word for society as such. Not at first. This God who presses His claim to all hearts has only *one* initial command: *Repent and believe the gospel.*

He never sends us to a derivative at the first. He never has us begin by reform or social service. He never begins with a lesser business than *repentance* and *belief*. The gospel has no other initial word.

The Golden Rule does not apply to you before this word has been received.

The Sermon on the Mount is not fit subject for your

study yet. All the marvelous social claims of the gospel ethic are not yours until you have repented and believed the gospel. He never sends us to a lesser business at the first. This is the Dayspring, *repentance* and *belief*, out of which pours all that is good in organized Christianity.

II

Yet men persist in some *false assumptions* that cover up this spring like my spring in the hills was covered. It is untrue:

that Christ has any message for unbelievers except "repent and believe";

that God exerts any claim on any man, state, or nation for "lip service";

that social and civic agencies and organizations can receive and pass on any of Christ by the mere repetition of certain of His teachings in their codes, bylaws, and creeds;

that governmental figures can acquire any merit from casual and occasional references to the guidance of Deity;

that the loyal support of any group, organization, or ideal that makes use of *any* of Christ's moral preachments as a substitute for personal surrender to the claims of Christ has any value whatever in enduring terms.

Who can in Christ's name say he believes anything Christ says who will not first believe Christ?

We have falsely assumed that the gospel message puts any requirements on any man ahead of its requirement to repent and believe. "Except ye believe that I am he," regardless of your cleanliness, regardless of your morality, your faithfulness, except you have made your personal surrender, believing surrender, "ye shall die in your sins."

Salvation—God's Lebensraum—room to live—the giving to man of his full integrity and health—is not to be found in pious impulses that send you to see the sick sometimes, nor in annual indications of your "moral" support at Easter and Christmas. Salvation is not to be found in your participation in community hymn singing, nor your holy-year pilgrimages, nor in the well-advertised "popular, bright, and breezy" services.

Christianity is not, and never was, a means of getting "good"; nor a useful ally for winning wars (Constantine's "Through this sign thou shalt conquer" to the contrary notwithstanding); nor a tool for maintaining national prosperity; nor a cult for the promotion of physical health, or the contact with departed spirits, or the prolongation of Anglo-Saxon domination. The "kingdom of heaven" never meant that or these.

It is out of *reliance on these wrong assumptions* that men frequently have given themselves to certain pseudo-Christian acts which replace the Dayspring.

They may rely upon their support of certain drives, programs, and community endeavors, good in themselves. For example, men may devote themselves to membership in certain organizations in America working at the race problem. A man can belong to all four hundred of them and still know no personal possession of the Spirit of Christ.

They will "learn the lingo," use the vocabulary of belief. They will even participate in worship and Christian action. Some, many, even go so far as to give gifts, generous gifts. Many men put great confidence in the worth of their observance of strict moral codes commonly thought to be "Christian" but actually "Stoic."

Thousands rely on a type of streamlined institutionalism that observes the amenities of traditional worship, illustrated by a church I saw advertising its *"Five-Minute Church Service for Folks in a Hurry."*

Sing one verse of a hymn.

Pray for thirty seconds.

Preach (?) for three and a half minutes.

and if you are in a hurry, you've had your shot for the week.

All this "Christianity"! It is typified in the quarterly "meeting" of the strictly limited social groups that make up the men's clubs of the suburban "church sets": long rows of thick-jawed, overstuffed, inventory-worried, high-blood-pressured, cardiac, successful young men, mingling at table with their blood brothers, and no others, over half-baked ham, watery green beans, sick apple slaw, and soggy pie, listening to anemic platitudes mouthed after dinner by some pale prelate who salts his sop with slang and stale jokes to hold their "interested," bored eyes. Then, to close the affair, "all join hands and *really* sing"—

Sweet fellowship, stirring beyond words! But isn't all this a far cry from that piercingly personal death warrant: "For God so loved the world that he gave his only begotten Son"?

The sum total of the lives based on these ridiculously ineffective assumptions is illustrated every week of the year in every city in the case of some citizen. Watch for it.

He is *prominent*—business or government, profession or politics, or property; at best a *surface* Christian; he is critically sick.[1]

The *doctor* will not tell him. He comes in smiling, so the patient won't know he is going to die.

The *friends* will not tell him. They mumble about how much "better" he looks than on yesterday's visit, so that he won't get the idea he is going to die.

The *preacher* mustn't go in—unless he is a very close friend; the man might think he is going to die.

The *wife*, meanwhile, does not tell him and is searching for insurance papers and will, which he likely does not have since it would have reminded him of his death.

[1] George A. Buttrick uses this figure here expanded to illustrate a basic point in *Christ and Man's Dilemma*, chap. IV.

Then he dies.

The *undertaker* tries his best to make him look not dead. The *friends* try to act as if he were only away. The *floral "offerings"* try to make it all bright and sunny. The *newspaper* lists all his accomplishments and organizations, as if they mattered; and only at the funeral must we stop our dodging and come to the truth: to wit, *this man is dead.*

Only at that moment, the moment of the funeral address, is the gospel permitted to speak in some lives.

It is too long delayed. He is dead. He can't find the Dayspring. For this man the gospel has no good news.

In one of Dorothy Sayers' plays Judas (another businessman of some prominence) speaks to the high priest following the great betrayal. "Do you know what hellfire is? It is the light of God's unbearable innocence that sears and shrivels you like flame. It shows you what you are. . . . Priest, it is a fearful thing to see one's self for a moment as one really is! I tell you, there is no escape from God's innocence."

All of us stand there. In the blazing light, God's innocence exerts its inalienable claim upon our lives.

The breadth of the thing is staggering. The burden of expressing the thing is beyond bearing. Who is sufficient to give words to it? Who can say it for so widely divergent a group in education, in background, in morals, belief, practice, gospel? Who can do it?

III

Is there *one* word for us all? And if there is, can a man find it and say it for you to hear?

For you who have found peace in Christ; for you who are on the border line of Christian peace and joy; for you who are struggling with temptation, often losing the victory; for you who are being overborne by illness, hardship, privation, misunderstanding, maladjustment, and sin; for you who are rebellious against God, against Christ, against His church, who are seeking to justify your selfish lives in enmity toward the Cross; for you who are helpless and hopeless, with dark minds and darker lives—is there *one* word for us all?

The New Testament knows nothing of averages. It has no average or mean between extremes. *Everyone* is of infinite value. But is there not *one* word that will fit us all?

Indeed! The just live, and by their faith.
Repent and believe this gospel.

REPENTANCE AND BELIEF = FAITH

Faith! That is the Word. The Dayspring. Faith!

There is no verb for it in English; there is no denial of it in experience. Our language breaks down. The one great act of the God-Man drama *has no word for the action.* At the one place a verb is needed we must use substantives—"repentance and belief." "To faith it."

To pitch out blindly on the darkness? No! No!

Rather, the free, responsible, chosen response of all that makes me person to the call of God's self-giving.

Faith! The just shall live—and by their faith. Repent and believe this good news.

Repentance? The one word that contains all essential ideas in the first stages of the Christian life. Waking from sleep; turning from idols.

Repentance? That change of mind in which I come to see my defection as God's innocence sees it.

Repentance? Reaction to sin as God reacts, a change of thought about sin and God, a change of feeling, a change of the will.

Repentance? Gift of the goodness of God, a permanent soul-attitude to self. A permanent moral process. A fixed habit of my soul.

Repentance? A turning of the will from the life and service of myself to the life and service of God.

Repentance? That that knows that anything contrary to God's will is contrary to my welfare. That that looks backward and forsakes—forward and accepts.

Belief—that hears as if it would obey once for all; that has no heart except for trust; that knows—at last—that a man meets God in God's Son—the Christ.

Belief that has learned that this good news can become my personal possession only in connection with a believing surrender to the Person of Jesus Christ.

Belief in one in whose presence one can afford to act as if trust were final and complete.

Belief with respect to Him who taught us to "faith" it.

Belief with respect to His ability to do what He said He could—forgive my sin, guide my destiny, bear my guilt, restore my soul, die and rise, lose and find, be broken and live.

Belief—I believe Him.

Repentance
> and
>> *Belief*
>>> make the verb = substantive
>>>> *Faith*.

Faith that encounters God, that appropriates his grace for its own. *Faith*—the first living cell of the Christian life, the root grace of all other graces. *Faith*—the universal requirement for Lebensraum, intensely personal and individual. *Faith*—that undergirds with enduring powers, that feeds on devotion and doubt.

The just shall live by faith. Child of my repentance—belief and God's grace.

And so one day in May, 1738, a sick, despairing little man went "very unwillingly" to a society in Aldersgate street where "one" was to read Luther's preface to the *Epistle to the Romans*. About a "quarter before nine" while "he" was describing the change which God works in the heart through faith in Christ:

Not that human notion and dream that some hold for faith . . . an idea in their hearts, which says, "I believe." . . .

Faith is . . . a divine work in us. It changes us and makes us
to be born of God. . . . It kills the old Adam, makes different
men in heart and spirit, mind, and power. . . . O, it is a living,
busy, active, mighty thing, this faith . . .

Then,
"I felt my heart strangely warmed."

. . . is a living, daring confidence in God's grace, so sure and
certain that a man would stake his life on it a thousand times.

And John Wesley closed the entry for that immortal
day in May with his own small hallelujah:
"But then I was sometimes, if not often, conquered;
Now, I was always conqueror!"
Perhaps he meant what John Masefield means: "Some-
thing above the wreck is always steady still."

GOD'S STRONG HANDS

CHAPTER FIVE

There is a message for
   all those who *in extremis* have sought
      to take life into their own fumbling
         hands.

And the message:
   Simply put, the gospel says that there is
no earthly cross before which a man must stop
and say "This is all; I can never pass this."
   God has strong hands to deal with crosses.

GOD'S STRONG HANDS

I

SOME OF THEM HAVE NO NAME IN MY MEMORY. I CAN'T
remember the name. I have no right to remember it. It
is good for them to know I can't remember when we
pass each other on the street. So some of them have no
name in my memory. Like anonymous letters there are
no names signed to the things they revealed in their
extremity.

Some of them gave me false names. They did not
know I can't remember anyway, but they knew that I
knew their name was assumed and we passed it by. The

things they were tortured to narrate to a stranger were true enough.

Some of them are just faces in my memory—disembodied, agonized, pulled up by their unanswerable dilemma. Some of them are just voices on a telephone. Voices in the night-time—occasionally drunken, always confused—never seen, only voices come to speak of their being held in the grip of manacles from the forge of their own smithy.

I remember a set of knuckles, bony and pale, almost bursting from the skin of the hands that gripped cell bars.

I remember a pair of tired old heels on high lace shoes, tapping, tapping out a tale of misery across and back from a door to a window.

I remember an ancient walking stick, rattling against the walls of a sour little room that enclosed and held frustrate its ancient inhabitant.

I remember hands—grubby, gnarled, nervous; I remember tendons swelling in a thin neck to raise a scarred head from a soiled bed in a back room. I remember the noxious fumes of cheap whisky and garlic around the long story "he" croaked out in a "Haymarket" mission.

Any pastor who has ever been asked, "What do you do all day?" by some well-adjusted friend showing his politeness can remember such faces, hands, feet, and the eyes—haunted, feverish eyes.

But he doesn't keep any list of them. The owners of those hands have a right to anonymity. Tragedy was not meant to be card-indexed in a file. Wreckage, human wreckage, is not subject to the confines of a catalogue. Not even God would do *that*. Let the heart keep the face and the trouble, and throw the name aside until he reminds you again. His story would likely be yours given the same torturing pressures.

So I remember them—all those dear people I have known who *in extremis* have sought to take life into their own fumbling hands—and just to them I sometimes must preach.

II

And the message?

Simply put, the gospel says that there is no possible earthly cross before which a man must stop and say "This is all; I can never pass this."

Simply put, the gospel says that God has strong hands to deal with crosses.

Simply put, the gospel says that a man must never let his disgust with the performance inveigle him into leaving before the play is over. If he should, he will miss the Resurrection that closes these episodes of Cross and Travail.

For: The gospel is no theoretical system of doctrine given for the occupation of theological minds.

The gospel is no philosophy of the universe given to compete with some "one-eyed" and abstract monism.

The gospel is not even doctrine except as it proclaims

79

the reality of God the Father in Jesus Christ, and even
that is just *given*.

Oh, how we have cluttered it up!

The gospel is no panacea for all troubles of the liver,
pancreas, thyroid, and hemoglobin. It is never cure-all
nor tonic.

Nor is the gospel a condiment to be sprinkled to taste
on the fat dishes served up by life to those who achieve
the proper combination of prosperity and humility,
frugality and philanthropy.

The gospel is simply the glad message that tells us of
life eternal in Jesus Christ. By treating of life eternal it
tells us how to live in life-present with all its crosses. It
talks of the soul, humility, mercy, and purity. It speaks
of the Cross and of the worthlessness of things.

Above all, it says, "Wait on God; see what He can
make of your defection. His strong hands work differently and most skillfully."

The gospel was given to assure you that in spite of
all your struggles something indestructible inside will
crown the gospel-led life in terms of peace and certainty.
There is no cross that certainty cannot pass. You must
not fail to catch this deep meaning of the gospel.

Once, even in thought, you give yourself to the con-
jecture that our gospel has no such deep meaning, that
moment you give yourself over to fatal passions within
which men live like animals, no restraint upon you ex-

cept your fear of other men made cruel by their fear of you.

Without this gospel-depth you are forced to lean on psychology, which has discovered that man is sick, but does not yet know he has been wounded by sin.

When you lose, even for a moment, this gospel-depth-of-assurance, then you are seized by *care*.[1] The care which Jesus compared to paganism; the care which makes us fearful slaves of today; the care which makes us fall prey to the world bit by bit; the care which Jesus felt an outrage against the great God who watches even sparrows and lilies; the care which gnaws at your vital relations with the Father, eats your childlike trust, rots your inmost soul, and winds you up in witless spiritual idiocy, pointless activity, hopeless confusion, beggarly self-pity, and bankrupt judgment.

The care which always issues in sensuality and leads us to try to get out of the prison we have made for ourselves by finding our god in some diverting process outside ourselves,[2] leads us to try to get out of the confusion sin has caused us by taking up new refuge in old flesh and its aged, unsatisfied appetites; that care which will always lead us sooner than late to the dread sin of *self-disgust*.

[1] Sören Kierkegaard, *passim*. Surprisingly, Harnack, *op. cit.*, has a great deal to give here.
[2] Reinhold Niebuhr, q.v. on sensuality in *The Nature and Destiny of Man*, I, 228-40.

Will you hear this? The gospel has a deep purpose: to bring men out of fatal passion, care, sensuality, and the sin of self-disgust, which is the sin of not loving one's self. Without this gospel purpose life becomes the foulest brew.

They look at me in unbelieving wonder when I tell them they must learn to love themselves. In the final analysis it is this self-disgust that sends those we remember to seek the help of men they trust. Self-disgust is the great culprit.

Have you heard it said of old-time, "Thou shalt not love thyself"? The gospel says to all those who fumble at life that there is a *self-love* which we ought to have in accordance with God's will. The gospel is your bulwark against the main force that produces human suffering—disgust with yourself, inability to love yourself. The last person on earth you will love is yourself. The last person on earth you will forgive a weakness is yourself. The last person on earth you will forgive an inability is yourself.

The Scripture says we must love our neighbors as ourselves. Then we must love ourselves, too—as God's creation, as God's image created anew.

Many people have lost this gospel meaning—or never had it. Many people do not love themselves at all; many feel a positive aversion to themselves. If a man does not love himself, he cannot forgive it to anyone. He will vent upon other people his bitterness against himself. It makes him touchy, proud, vindictive, haughty, surly. Oh, the things a man will do to those he loves out of his bitter dissatisfaction with himself!

Outside the gospel which one of us can go on loving, forgiving himself? You have found out already how unlovable you are to yourself? Aside from this gospel life becomes that foul brew of self-disgust.

The meaning of this gospel for this day's journey is this: *Only in the gospel can men go on loving themselves. Wait on God! See what His strong hands will fashion out of your defection.*

David did not wait to see what God's strong hands would make of his sin with Bathsheba. It was self-disgust as much as anything else that sent that cursed letter to Joab.

Moses did not wait on God's strong hands, and it was self-disgust that smote the rock and barred him from Canaan.

Elijah, seized by self-disgusting fear, could not wait for God's strong hands and ran a hundred miles to get away from Jezebel at Shechem.

And Judas did not wait. What an encounter if he had! But Judas did not give God's strong hands a chance—life had turned sour, fermented, blown up. He could no longer love himself, and Judas knew far ahead of Oscar Wilde that

> Each narrow cell in which we dwell
> Is a foul and dark latrine,
> And the fetid breath of living Death
> Chokes up each grated screen,
> For all, but Lust, is turned to dust
> In Humanity's machine.

Whoever saw a man who looked "with such a wistful eye" upon what he had done and wished so earnestly that he had not done it?

So Judas hanged himself. Thereby, as Dorothy Sayers says it, Judas committed the final, the fatal, the most pitiful error of all—for he missed the gospel meaning; he despaired of God and himself; he never waited to see *resurrection*.[3]

Had he waited, had he not taken life into his own hands, had he waited to see what God's strong hands could do, had he stayed on stage as the script commanded, there would have been a meeting—Jesus and Judas—an encounter to leave our imagination gasping at its potential.

The gospel message is this: Wait on God! Let Him make what He will of your weakness.

Judas saw the dreadful payment made and never knew what victory had been purchased with the price. But the final tragedy of Judas was not his betrayal, nor was it

[3] Dr. Charles Pierce called my attention to this idea and others in Sayers, *op. cit.*

his love of money, nor of power, nor was it his "political idealism." The final tragedy was that he did not wait to see what the strong hands of God would do to his defection. He failed to wait for *resurrection*. He despaired of God and himself; he left before the play was over. He missed the final curtain. *He forgot that God can swallow weakness.*

For you to ask, "Why, if God's hands are so strong, does God not smite all evil dead?" is a question far removed from this. Better ask why He did not strike you dumb before you uttered that baseless and unkind slander day before yesterday.[4] Or better ask why He did not strike you paralytic before you submitted to the claims of that fleshly temptation. Or why He did not turn me imbecile before some shoddily prepared sermon is allowed to fall on an eager ear.

III

Oh, God's strong hands work differently! He takes our sins and our errors and turns them into victories. He makes Crucifixion's crime into world salvation. He twists the crown of thorns into a crown of glory. "O felix culpa!" cried Augustine—"Oh, happy guilt of mine! *Oh, marvelous defection that doth deserve so great a Redeemer!*"

The disciples had misunderstood nearly everything

[4] *Ibid.*

that Christ had said to them, but now since Resurrection it didn't matter. It all added up. It made sense with a meaning far beyond their wildest hopes. Christ in the strong hands of God conquering my defection. This is the gospel.

For these men a means had been found to look upon His face and live. They had seen God's eternal face turned upon them in their defection and self-disgust, and because the face of God was that of a "suffering and rejoicing man," they knew themselves safe in His strong hands.

And they were persuaded that life is worth living, that death is a triviality. They had found a way to conquer care, to process passion, to overrule sensuality. Now they could love themselves and all other of God's creatures.

When a man waits to see what God can make of his defection, in the strong hands of God the *cross* becomes a *throne*, the *crown of thorns* twists into a *glory*, the solid back of a *sepulcher* becomes a *gateway*.

In God's strong hands *exit* is *entrance*, *death* is *life*, *mourning* is *laughter*.

The *Nazarene* is *international*, fanatic *Saul* is giant *Paul*, *pain* becomes *pathway*, *lostness* is made *salvation*, the great *dread* becomes the grand *victory*, *defeat* becomes *conquest*, *loss* becomes great *gain*, the great *burden* —the great *opportunity*.

The Church in travail becomes the Church at rest; the meetinghouse on the corner becomes the heart of civilization. Little Palestine becomes the focal center of earth, and in God's strong hands publishers rush to print words said by a man named Schweitzer lost in a jungle.

In God's strong hands *last* becomes *first*, and *least* is *greatest*. This is gospel.

Wait and see what God's strong hands will make of your weakness. Then you can love yourself again.

I know a friend who, where she lies, is trying the best she knows to mount up on enough strength to be able to endure the rest of this pain-racked day. Dear friend, wait and see what God will make of that pain.

I have other friends who face today in their own hearts the tremendous, eroding waste of a great washing grief. Wait! See what God will make out of grief. Look what He made of betrayal—a *resurrection*.

And to that little friend of mine whom life has blocked from every door and window—she has no peace inside, and life can express itself only by slapping back at each day as she lives it. Wait! He can fix frustration too, and bored loneliness, and misery, and misfittedness.

And to that other friend of mine. Wait! Call a thousand times if you need to, but wait. See what God means to make of your self-disgust.

The sin of Judas was that he forgot that Jesus along with Judas' sin was in the strong hands of God. And I forget. Nearly every day I forget—and when I remember, I cry,

> "O God, help me to wait and see—
> There is so much defection,
> Such critical weakness,
> here, inside.
> Save me from self-disgust.
> I wait for Thy strong hands to
> Make what they will
> of my defection."

IV

"Name of God!" he swore in shock and delirium. "If I could get to that river, I'd fix this mess." And in my own heart almost I could have helped him get there if it would have fixed it—but it wouldn't have changed anything. In my ignorance I thought not even God could fix it—foolish youth.

Down an orderly hall, along another corridor, another day, dying brown eyes whose name I can't remember and whose depth I can't forget pleading, "Don't let my family see me—yet."

Huge bulk wallowing on thick carpet, wild eyes not too wild to recognize doctor and pastor, hoarse voice shouting, "Why in the —— did you send for them? Am I gonna die? Am I gonna die?"

Calm voice, cultured voice, influential voice, coming

up out of pain: "I sent for you—I don't know how to pray."

White knuckles below red wrists tensely gripping bed rail—sergeant's stripes, Scandinavian shoulders, fixed eyes glued to a sick little body while a Catholic nun and a preacher pray.

Whisky bottle bulging side pocket; weepy, bleary eyes; voice of self-pity drooling its woes: "Sure, I roughed her up a little—God knows I didn't mean to do *that* to her. But I can't give up the kids."

Loyal, devoted, poverty-stricken, forsaken, at the end of her row—I remember her.

Betrayed, penniless, crippled—I remember him. His brother was a famous preacher in a faraway place.

Compromised, seduced, no answer but a criminal one they thought—I remember them. Across the years and the pastorates I remember them.

The point is that *God does too.*

Melodrama? Tinted by imagination? Dreamed-up emotional binge? Bid for sympathy? Scum of the earth? Riffraff getting what they deserve? Tales told by an overwrought fanatic?

Not on your life! Rather, the cross section of memory of any honest workman in any kind of pastorate through any ten-year span of life.

And the point is that *God remembers them too.*

There is a message for them and for all those whose fumbling hands pluck at life's coverlet.

89

PART TWO

CHORUS

The Gospel in Christ
for All Mankind

CHAPTER SIX

He knew then, Satan knew, what He meant to do to human
  personality: that He meant to make Man free:
    free to meet his Redeemer by a free choice,
      a free responsible choice; choice of
        a spiritual condition that makes
          a kingdom of heaven possible.

Satan knew—they all knew very well. Satan and his evil spirits
and Pilate understood it. They had to reject Him.
  Their dominions would be swallowed up by freed men.
  The dominion of demons would die.
    The empire of the Romans would become a
      vassal state to a Judean King of Kings.
    They *had* to reject!

Caiaphas! *Hurry!* You are a year too late already.

HIS ENEMIES UNDERSTOOD

I

AMONG HIS DISCIPLES WHO HAS EVER UNDERSTOOD HIM?
The most bewildered and confused men on earth must
have been His disciples.

When a highly to be desired young prince came to join
Him, He sent him away sorrowing. When the crowds
at last began to follow Him, He turned away grieving.
(*Isn't this what you wanted, Master? Now, oh, why do
you grieve that they follow?*)

In violation of all social and religious codes He sat at
a well to talk to a *woman*—and a *Samaritan* woman at
that! To the accompaniment of wild hosannas, He in-

sisted on riding a *donkey*. Social opportunities that would have given prestige He twisted into nothing—as when at a rich man's house He spent His time talking to a sinner woman who wandered in. They could not understand Him.

He went to share the grief of Mary and Martha, even wept at their weeping—then stood before their dead man's tomb and called the dead man out.

They could not grasp Him—they could not understand this remarkably remarkable Person. "How strange!" they said among themselves.

"He speaks of going away, having told us we must follow Him always—then says we cannot follow Him now."

"He speaks of a Father of Abraham as if He had seen Him—when everyone knows that Terah died, sidetracked in Haran, centuries ago."

"He talks of a Kingdom—but will ride only a donkey and rejects a crown."

"He speaks of His death—yet acts as if He would be with us always."

"We cannot follow it. He is beyond our understanding." And so Judas fell before it; Peter collapsed and denied; Thomas was twisted by his love and his wonder.

Yet His enemies understood. They had little difficulty grasping Him. They knew as little of Him as did His disciples, but they knew He was dangerous.

Did I say "enemies"? How incongruous that He should

have enemies! This gentle, forgiving, mercifully mild Teacher. No *teacher* is dangerous. How utterly harmless He is!

He talks so easily and so quietly of turning other cheeks, of giving away coats, of sparrows, and lilies, and grass, and vines, and branches, of bread and water, and peace inside you, of two miles for one, of loving enemies, and of meekness, and mercy, and purity, and light, and salt.

Now whoever heard of talk about *purity* being dangerous? How utterly harmless to talk about saintliness! No one could object to that.

But one day Annas, high priest, heard Him say, "I and my Father are one."

Somewhere in the back of that priestly head a little bell rang. Such a man is dangerous. That would wipe out the priesthood. Who would need *us* if men could *feel* God and *see* Him? The priesthood would come down like a collapsed tent. And Annas was high priest and wouldn't like that.

Scribes heard Him when He said, *"The sabbath was made for man, and not man for the sabbath."* They were not fools. They knew what He meant. Personality is paramount. In any conflict of personality (freeborn) and law it is person that matters. They knew full well what this would do to professional writers of religious law, and no scribe could like that.

Pharisees were there and heard Him say, *"Broad is the way to destruction. Unless your righteousness go beyond that of scribes and Pharisees—unless it be of different stuff —you are unfit."* They—*Pharisees*—must submit to this? They, the best men Judaism could make, must hear sinners put above themselves? Publicans set ahead of the pious? The unclean above the clean? Those outside the law above those within the law? The last above the first? The perishing over the saved? The wicked above the good? They were driven frantic by this new system of value that denied their pious patterns. They understood Him.

Talk about lilies—dangerous? Yes, lilies, and flowers, and drying hay in the meadows—dangerous.

And Pilate? Pilate heard Him plainly when He said, "My kingdom is not of this world," and felt a great relief. But Pilate also heard Him say, *"Thou [Pilate] couldest have no power at all, except it were given thee from above."* And Pilate then knew there was no god for him but Caesar. All Caesars know that, and all of Caesars' governors know it. This Man, then, must die!

Even the evil spirits knew Him for what He was and cried from their home in an insane man, *"Let us alone, Thou Son of God! What have we to do with Thee?"*

And Satan? When Satan heard Him say, "Man shall not live by bread alone. . . . Thou shalt not tempt the Lord thy God. . . . Get thee behind!" he knew then,

Satan knew, what He meant to do to human personality:
  that He meant to make Man free:
    free to meet his Redeemer by a free choice,
      a free responsible choice; choice of
        a spiritual condition that makes
          a kingdom of heaven possible.
Satan knew—they all knew very well. Satan and his evil
spirits and Pilate understood it. They had to reject Him.
  Their dominions would be swallowed up by freed men.
    The dominion of demons would die.
      The empire of the Romans would become a
        vassal state to a Judean King of Kings.
      , They *had* to reject!
Caiaphas! *Hurry!* You are a year too late already.

And so with scribes and Pharisees and priests, the best
of Hebrew culture—their dominions would be swallowed
too. Priests, law, patterns of their piety, dogma of their
orthodoxy, all would go by the board—jettisoned, for
who would worship through a dependent priest in a man-
made temple when he had the Lord Himself? Who
would live by law when He lifts one above law? Who
would confine himself to a pattern when He has the
original?

They knew Him well—better than did His disciples.
They had to reject Him, for Jewish culture would have
died. "Let Him be crossed!" they shouted. And it was
for them the only way.

II

But *What His enemies did not know* was that everything really Jewish, all that is eternal of Jewry, was wrapped up in what happened to this Teacher. They never in their wildest dreams dreamed that He could escape and outlive Jewish culture and become universal. They never dreamed that twenty centuries later a Dutchman, descendant of a tribe of then wild German barbars, would petition the supreme court of a new and entirely changed culture called Israel to open the old case of Jesus of Nazareth.

They did not know that He could not remain on their cross, that Rome's cross could not keep Him, that no one can cross Messiah, not so He stays crucified. Messiahs do not wilt under death—they climb aboard it and make of it a chariot. They turn the spilled blood of Medusa into Pegasus and put a bridle on him. They did not know about Messiahs and death, and war horses with wings made out of death. But the centurion who crossed Him and watched Him die knew, and "as the air grew conscious of a God and raptures unenjoyed and pleasures dead, and all the pain of things unsatisfied, came 'round his dying head," the centurion knew and said, *"Truly this was the Son of God."*

You can't crucify Messiah. *Not so He stays that way. But we have expected His cross to hold Him, too,* and are thunderstruck when for a little He is inadvertently freed.

In our misunderstanding we have tried our best to keep Him there. We make Him a white man, member of the tribe, national, citizen, partisan, bigot moralist, or ascetic monk, or legalist reactionary, a Baptist, and a Texan, if you please. May God forgive us.

Our neighbor, six years of age with all that means, was looking through an old color book smeared by our "littlest." In her ignorance the three year old had colored the flag of the United States and its forty-eight stars orange and green and yellow. Our neighbor almost gave me a sermon when she cried, "Oh, no, it's all wrong! that's the Texas flag, and everyone knows it's red, white, and blue."

"That's the Texas Christ," we cry, or the Baptist, or the American, or the white, "and you must hold Him as we do!" In our concentration on explaining and defending His cross we have expected the cross to go on holding Him. We see only by the hardest that He is infinitely greater after His cross simply because men could not comprehend that there could be any afterward for a man on a cross.

His "afterward" is greater than His approach to the cross. But the cross was finished, and even as He cried, "Tetelestai," the "Author of all things," to use a sentence of Paul Scherer's, "drew a line through all the contradictions and wrote across the original text with His own hand—*stet*. Let it stand! Let it stand forever."

Yet we have expected His cross to hold Him. If He is not free to roam the hidden roads of our hearts, it is easier to escape.

Once a man frees Him from that cross, *He becomes embarrassingly divisive* and sets a child against the father. Released from His stanchion, *He becomes uncomfortably selfish;* for no man can serve Him and another.

It is this fear of His release in our lives that makes us party to His death. It is our guillotinade—our doing— for we hear that off His cross He is unaccountably jealous, "if ye believe not that I am he"; He is compellingly single-minded, "I and my Father are one"; He is disturbingly disruptive and came "not to send peace, but a sword." Freed from that cross He is eternally personal. Kept to that beam He is personally tragic. (How strange, says Berdyaev, that the religion of the cross should deny tragedy!) So, seeking escape from His possessiveness and His personalness, we have caged Him. He is less disruptive left on His cross.

How we have caged Him! Not knowing that He is beyond *good* and *evil* because above law to grace; beyond *father* and *mother* because above dependence to trust; beyond the *limits of race* because above kinship or kind to unity; beyond *national barriers* because above Caesar to Jehovah; beyond *religious prejudice* because

100

above schism to freedom; beyond mere *orthodoxy* because above doctrine to communion; beyond the *institutional* because above pattern to original.

How pathetically funny that *in caging Him we have confined ourselves!* In our fear of His release to do His transforming work in our lives we have built for ourselves a mare's nest of a cage into which He could not come if He would. Hiding from Him behind programs and plans, standards and organizations, bars of ritual and petty dogma and all the externals of institutionalism, so that His brotherhood-of-believing-hearts has become largely in our day a fat old lady, sitting in a rock-ribbed castle, counting war bonds.

The Church has disguised itself from Him, and in order to keep Him away hires *pastors*, of whom its members frequently make *beggars*, to finance our own little kingdom; or *gigolos*, to charm our society friends in voice and manner when they come around to see God occasionally; or even *slave drivers*, if by chance we are big enough and the people are little enough; *share-cropper* tenants, here for a little while to tend crops not our own until the will of the owner sends us to other fields not our own; or, more frequently, we let them make us *plumbers*, suction pump in hand, unclogging stopped channels of grace all the ministry long, so elated when after months of effort some "believer" begins to act like what he said he was years before; or glorified *glass blowers*, busy with bellows, and fire and glass, and breath, blowing our col-

101

lapsed religion back into color and shape again; or better, in dodging Him we have made our spiritual leaders to be *bellwethers*, by which I mean that as pastor I am quite frequently expected to be a sexless sort of old goat who by ringing bells and bleating leads the sheep into the right pen for the slaughter *"in nomine Domini Jesu Christi"* and in the name of *religion.*

How we have tamed Him (and ourselves and our pastors in the process)! *We have kept Him safely shut up in church* (Jesus is never very dangerous in church, you know), when He was always free in the streets. *We have kept Him enclosed, shielded from commerce;* but He was ever in the markets with men. *We have sought to keep Him wrapped in a napkin with the host or in wine,* when all He ever wanted was to get into a man's blood stream. *We have limited Him to dealing with sin only,* when He preferred to start with darkness, or lameness, or demons, or need, and let sin die as He passed it. *We have protected Him against being taken seriously with armored dogma,* while He never guarded His words against misunderstanding. *We have provided Him with a round of philosophies,* but all He ever wanted was someone to trust Him. *We have ensconced Him safely in niches where He is worshiped,* but He preferred boats and houses and street corners and Solomon's pool.

How we have caged Him! Behind bars of dogma, when He rejects confinement. Behind the walls of institutionalism, while He cries for the brotherhood of believing ones. How we have forced Him to peer through slatted apertures into tiny apartments made up for company, when He would roam the whole dwelling!

III

Who has learned it? He divides; He monopolizes; He compels; He disrupts. Free Him from the cross where you have wanted to keep Him. Strike the shackles, bend the bars, destroy the confinement of your church—prison house, and let Him wander in you redeeming in the streets, as of old. Let Him divide you, monopolize you, use you.

When will we ever learn it? Jesus is the *life*—and life is *truth* and *way*—and truth can free us from our incompetence, and our shoddy work, and our own insipidity that often "creates a boredom like to that of hell." We are still a proud and foolish, blind people.

He wants us a freely working power along the avenue, not clustered for refuge like quail on a cold day. He wants us grown beyond good and evil, not seeking decay in our neighbors like green flies on a carcass. He wants us unbound, stricken of fetters, a redeeming people, because we are beyond slavery to ideas and dead dogma, ourselves redemptive, as He was redemptive. He wants us redeemers in Austin as in Asia, in Texas as in Tunisia.

So many there are among us who know all about the

insufficiencies of earth, but to save their souls, cannot find heaven. They will never find Him until we free Him from His cross and let Him go to them in us.

Perhaps even now you are saying, "I shall do it!" And in a moment when you go out the door, down the steps, and away from the power of this particular moment, you will begin to say, "I made my decision, but where shall I begin?"

Immediately there will come to your mind's eye the picture of untouched thousands in your city, then the cities beyond that—and beyond that—and that—and the enormity of the thing will cover you up, and you will cry, "How can I begin anywhere?"

God requires only that we start where we are. Free Him! Whatever He says to your heart, do it. Free Him to walk on the streets as He wants to walk. Free Him to move in a man's bloodstream as he wants to move. Free Him to possess the heart of a child as He wants to possess it.

Come down, Son of Man!
Come down from Thy cross
And walk amongst us,
for
We would understand Thee.

SEND THEM AWAY, LORD

CHAPTER SEVEN

The fires are all dead. The glow from the ashes is gone. Christianity is alone. And her garrisons are asleep like the tame geese Kierkegaard called us, roosting wing to wing in long rows on roosts, upholstered roosts. Alone and asleep.

"Send them away, Lord!" the disciples cried. *"Pronounce the benediction and let's go home. It's too late. The day is far along. Dismiss with a word of prayer, Lord. Pronounce a little blessing. Church is out."*

But listen! Listen! The Church of Jesus has stood in many desert places.

SEND THEM AWAY, LORD

I

*"Awake, thou that sleepest, and arise from
the dead, and Christ shall
shine upon thee."*

What a day this is to be awake! And what a day to sleep!
Preaching for today's world is largely a business of
awakening the sleeping giants in the churches. Yet this
awakening must never be done too brusquely, for in the
Upanishads of ancient India is it not taught for all the
faithful that when a man sleeps, his soul leaves him?
Therefore it is a rule:

"Let no one wake a man suddenly,
    for it is a matter difficult of cure
if his soul find not its way back to him."

So as gently as possible (to run no risk of inciting soulless giants to further soulless and fruitless activity), yet as firmly as necessary (to run no risk of remaining asleep and hence disunited and witless in the face of danger), let me insist that the most appalling task facing any group on earth is that task now facing the Christian churches. Christianity must now stand alone.

In a snidely clever remark Bertrand Russell meant to sting when he said, "A great majority of the human race have religious convictions different from our own, and therefore groundless." Let me show you why he speaks the truth.

The thirteen hundred years from 650 B.C. to A.D. 650 literally flamed with religious promise. In that comparatively compact package of time came to flower all the currently "well-heard-of" religions: those of Buddha, Confucius, the Christ; Mani, Mohammed, Zoroaster; the mystery cults, the best of Greek philosophy, and Christianized Neo-Platonism; Judaism, Jainism, Taoism; Shintoism and, largely, Hinduism. And these for the most part remain. How now can it be claimed that *Christianity stands alone?* [1]

It has been five hundred years since Buddhism advanced

[1] See Latourette's fine analysis, *op. cit.*, pp. 1-19.

internally or externally. Neither creatively nor geographically can it be made to go forward. It is finished. For a thousand years Buddhism has been a declining power in China.

It has been 750 years since Confucianism produced its last outstanding figure, Chu Hsi; and his attempt to combine Taoism, Buddhism, and Confucianism never really came off. For what was to be the mother matrix, Confucianism, needed the Chinese imperial system to feed upon. When it died, Confucianism lost its oxygen supply.

Manichaeism has disappeared. Mohammedanism has not passed the peak it reached nine hundred years ago.

Zoroastrianism's Mazda is now an electric light globe, and her god of evil then spelled "Ahriman" has now appeared in Persian eyes to be the great American negotiator Harriman.

The mystery cults have been dead for fourteen hundred years. Even their vocabulary is gone except to a Frenchman named Cumont, a few old texts in ecclesiastical history, and the ritual writers of secret fraternal orders. Not even the members know the words they use.

Neo-Platonism died seventeen hundred years ago except for the resurrection of some of its claims in modern Christian Science.

For a thousand years Judaism has produced no towering figure nor any major stimulus. Taoism has been a minor religion fifteen hundred years.

The fires are all dead. The glow from the ashes is gone.

109

Christianity is alone. And her garrisons are asleep like the tame geese Kierkegaard called us, roosting wing to wing in long rows on roosts, upholstered roosts. Alone and asleep.

II

And alone Christianity must now face some terribly powerful forces: revolutions, new ideologies, the grasping state power, the "scientific" approach to life, nontheistic humanisms, ever-rising new secularisms, vast shifts in populations, dislocations of standards, new wars. We live now in a "fulness of the time."

Amidst sweeping revolutions an old world labors to let a new world live. The child of her travail has inborn new and radical ideas about many things: the universe, society, Man.

Mixed in the blood stream of the new world, shifting and changing, tormenting and questioning, denying and affirming, forcing her to seek new kinds of food by the hungers built up, is a set of genes, a heterogeneous collation of globules, drawn from the spinal fluid under the brains of Karl Marx, Friedrich Nietzsche, Sigmund Freud, Charles Darwin, Albert Einstein, and John Dewey. Enough to make the blood of this new world green.

Further, we live in an age in which the state reasserts itself as a new-old menace, in which our new tools have already become vicious masters, in which our great blasphemy is that we make ourselves gods and our God the tool of the party in power, in which our great danger lies in our great popularity and our strength becomes but a guard to protect the extant order.

We live in an age of unparalleled numerical growth accompanied by an unparalleled spiritual illiteracy, complicated by our numerical neuroses and organized superficialities. An age of grasping competition, biased convictions, rival theories, clashing ideologies, matter-mad human bugs, activism, preoccupation, and thrusting disregard for human values. Through such a welter must the churches wade, even in my town, along with *certain specific challengers which face my church like hungry children face a bewildered parent.*

Twenty-six pages, foolscap size, with names packed from edge to edge, representing the several thousand unhelped university students alone; the deracinated hordes of the unwon who have established almost no community ties of any kind, who live out existences of work and amusement without assuming any responsibility whatever for our community and its spirit; at least six more major areas of the city, in addition to Montopolis, Northwest, Allandale, and Wilshire Wood, needing churches, pastors, and Sunday schools; the claims of needy sister churches; the great schools which my church upholds; the missions in Argentina and China; orphans, indigents, dependents; hundreds of homes on the rolls where the work has made little appeal; more than a thousand children needing

111

understanding example, instruction, undergirding; the four hundred loyal teachers and helpers who need tools, encouragement, heightened vision; the one hundred young married couples whose homes need a pastor and a church and many friends; the scores of aged and faithful who deserve a special ministry; the silently suffering ones no one knows are hurting; the triteness of the institutional approaches; outworn concepts and prejudices; the numerical neurosis that insists so many more noses must be counted than last year to stay in business; the spiritual lethargy, wasted energy, and duplicated effort. The claims of a capital city. The claims of a lost city. The claims of a cultural center—*and the paradox:*

Though responsible for all, *we can never take all.* Though wanting all, *we are ever unfulfilled* till He comes. Forever seeking—forever unsatisfied with what we find.

"It is too much!" we cry. "The Church cannot do it. Send them away, Lord!" That is our age-old answer. It is too much. The day is far passed. Night is falling. Send them away.

Even in the New Testament this answer was used. Word that John the Baptist had died brought to Jesus an urgent desire to be away from it all. Sorely He needed rest and prayer. Part of Himself had died in the beloved Forerunner, and his bloody death brought the Master's cross very close for a while. But there was no escape from the pressing of the people. Not yet. They even followed along the shore when He attempted to travel by boat.

Multitudes followed the little ship, seeking, seeking, more of this new thing, or more healing, or just a glimpse of Beyond.

Mark tells us how compassion for them at last pulled Jesus into shore at a desert place where He taught them through the day. But day's end came, and in that wild desert setting a strange unrest possessed the multitude: the cry of unfed babies, the petulant wailing of exhausted children, the complaints of spent mothers, the mutterings of tired, sullen fathers—aimlessly milling, milling, like cattle ready for stampede. The situation was out of hand. The job was too big for the Church. Something had to be done—but it was too big.

"Send them away, Lord!" the disciples cried. *"Pronounce the benediction and let's go home. It's too late. The day is far along. Dismiss with a word of prayer, Lord. Pronounce a little blessing. Church is out."*

But the Church of Jesus is constantly up against things too big to be handled even as now. Historically, and too often, our only action has been to call for the benediction and go home. Send them away, Lord!

We did it. "It's too big!" we cried.

While slavery of human beings was splitting us open, while land-grabbers legislated a noble red race out of existence, while crime and vice were becoming major business, when war was declared by a newspaper publisher, and a generation later when narrow minds in high places barred us from a real seat with the League of

Nations and killed a crusader named Wilson, we did it again. But why speak of a generation gone? We are doing it now.

Send them away, Lord! The day is far passed. Pronounce the benediction and send us home. The Church can't deal with it. It's too big.

The matter of still subjugated races, the matter of legalized corruptions, the matter of almost complete moral defection, the secularization of all that is spiritual, the matter of mass drunkenness, mass dope addiction, mass pandering, mass legal pilfering, mass rule by minority pressure, mass murder by auto, mass suicide by gluttony, mass insanity by alcoholism, mass prostitution for peanuts, mass strangulation on patented pills; plus the little matters of our own veneered hates, spiritual dishonesty, squeezing acquisitiveness, backyard prejudices and sectional provincialism; plus our own little bigotries, shallowness, high tempers, lack of pity, lack of mercy, and lack of gentleness.

III

But listen! Listen! The Church of Jesus has stood in many desert places. When Jerusalem was plunged into a basin of blood by Titus; when the Vandals hammered in all of North Africa's gates; when the wolves and the Magyars owned all France; when Turks and Crusaders made Eurasia slippery with shed blood; when priests despoiled their own altar cloths; when a hundred thou-

114

sand believers died in that day at Vespers; when eighteen out of thirty million Germans died in that useless thirty-years war; in plague-ridden Moscow when two hundred and fifty thousand died; and in Lenin-ridden Russia where eighteen million starved; in quake-shaken Japan and in German-raped Belgium, *the Church has stood in many desert places.* And all too often in the face of its task has the cry been raised in despair—the task is too big—*"From the fury of the Northmen, good Lord, deliver us!* Send them away, Lord! This is a desert place, and the day is far spent."

Indeed! It is a desert place—this avenue to a new age. Indeed! The task that confronts us is larger than we are. Indeed! The temptation is to cry: "Send them away! The stability of our own future is questionable. We've scarcely what we want for our own. We have other commitments. We have heard enough of need, conflict, danger, crisis, challenge, and obligation. Send them away, Lord! It is toward evening; it is getting dark."

What the whole Christian world has forgotten is that in response to the need of that milling multitude and in the face of the disciples' plea for a benediction that would relieve them of their responsibility *Jesus had an express command in answer.*

"Give ye them to eat!" ("My Father wants them fed!")

And the disciples are aghast.

"You play with us, Lord."

"You jest."

"You know it's too big."

"How could we feed them?"

"The Lord is not in earnest. He wouldn't require such of us."

"Why, Lord, it would take all our money! Two-hundred-days-work worth wouldn't do it. It would break us up."

"If God wants them fed, where is heaven's manna?"

"If God wants them fed, where are heaven's ravens?"

"If God wants this world, where are heaven's armies?"

"*You* are heaven's raven with meat in your pinions. *You* are heaven's manna falling in showers of life. *You* are the armies of heaven."

"But, Lord, we have so little! Only five small loaves and two little fish," says Andrew, and adds with failing faith, "What are they among so *many?*"

"*Give me what you have!*" And it is a trumpet sound, more felt than heard. "Give me your loaves and the fish. Under my control it is enough."

The Christian world has forgotten—He asks for nothing we do not already have. The Christian world has forgotten—anything we still have is left over from our own needs. Give Him what you have. We have forgotten that under His control *it is enough.*

We have forgotten that old Isaiah said the day would come when we would have our chance, that Yahweh-worship would be all that remained. We have forgotten that the gospel is eternal—never needing any defense. We have forgotten that only forms of Christianity can die—the gospel never. Only Christianity's dwelling can be in danger. Only Christianity's institutions are perishable. Only the habiliments are inflammable. The gospel has no bulwark or bastion; it is never on defense, and we have forgotten it.

Around us corpses—dead and half-dead earthly forms. Eastern Orthodoxy progressively reflects an era gone. The Roman communion restricted its papal chair to men of Italy now four centuries ago, and that day hastened its death. The state churches of Europe choke on their admission of multitudes by virtue of having been born once only. The Protestant communions exhaust their spiritual energy building one more great refuge for defense in spite of the preachment that it is a base for attack.

And our own? Smothering under our claims of "big numbers," "winning the world" through the front door and passing it out the back to make room inside, glossing over our failures with braggadocio, flashing shields of brass that once were gold, riding our crest of popularity at home gloating over our unbrotherliness abroad, defiantly clamant for the "seat on his right hand"—sinning like James and John in asking for it before we are "able."

Dissipating our strength in hasty expansion, our future in unbrotherly provincialism, our honor in boorish assumptions, our heritage for a mess of pottage; building

117

barns, stores for perishable products; erecting defenses when we were born for assault; enrolling without winning; counting without converting; penning up without feeding the flock; washing without water; teaching without vision. *What confession we need!*

Whoever told us it was our fight alone? Whoever said the Church was hemmed in, beseiged? We are not a surrounded city; we are a beseiging army. An army of many divisions against which the gates of the place of the abandoned cannot stand.

Whoever said it was our business to survive or to remain unchanged, or to count and compare, or to huddle up in refuges for defense? Whoever gave us permission to try to bind the fresh ferment of the gospel in the wineskins of the dead past? Whoever released us to wrap our gospel in graveclothes for safekeeping?

We have forgotten our Commander never defends. We have forgotten our gospel cannot be smothered. We have forgotten the gospel will always split any force that confines it, until it threatens to split us. We have forgotten that Jesus is with us. We have mistaken our plan for His own. We have assumed the regency. But He is here. He needs only our soldiership, not our generalship. We have forgotten it. He wants only what we have. Under His control the gospel does its own multiplying. Under His control it is enough.

And then, in view of the thousands, surrounded by a knot of disciples agape, in the presence of God's gospel, then the very air grew conscious of a God as with five loaves and two fish He *multiplied* to meet the need around Him.

Awake, thou that sleepest! He asks only for what you already have. Under His control it is enough.

> Sing louder yet,
>> Why must I still behold the wan white face
>>> Of that deserted Christ,
> Whose bleeding hands my hands did once enfold,
>> Whose smitten lips my lips so oft have kissed,
> And now in mute and marble misery,
>> Sits in His lone deserted house and weeps,
>>> Perchance for me.

Is it because I have not yet given Him what I have? Under His control *it is enough*, and He feeds them with our fish.

CHAPTER EIGHT

I know of a warden in Georgia, and a jury in South Carolina.
 I know about salt in the soup at Rochester,
 and no red men in white men's graves in Iowa.
I saw a Jew berate a Negro porter for trying
 to help him in the airport at Knoxville.
I have heard about bombs in Dallas and mobs in Cicero.
I have seen bedraggled white children sitting on
curbs outside movie palaces and grocery stores.
 I saw GIs turned away from shoddy
 hovels because they had children.
 I've watched the "line-up" in police
  courts on Monday morning, and I have
 ridden in squad cars on Sunday nights.
  I know about drunk Mexicans,
  and hungry sneak thieves, and the
   powerful clause "Caucasian only"
   in deeds and contracts.

I know about railroad tracks and inheritances,
  share croppers and tenants.
 I have heard Black Maria's scream as she
  roared down Madison to pick
  up a load of flotsam.
 I have heard the "thwack" as a club
met a head outside where I preached in the slums.
I have smelt the fourth floor of a broken-down
  tenement—and I tell you, my Master did
   not intend *this*.
 Whatever Jesus intended, it was not *this*.
Our brother's blood crieth out from the ground.

ALL THE SONS OF EARTH

I

HOW COURAGEOUSLY, AND WITH WHAT JOYOUS ABANDON, our more liberal-minded pastors have beat us over the head with our failures to live in unprejudiced freedom.

I have done it myself—preening myself piously before my cracked mirror that I have had courage to say something about prejudice when I should have done something long before.

It's almost too late to preach about it. Yet all along there have been those who did more doing than preaching. Let me come at it from a different direction.

Let me insist that in spite of all appearance Christian

people have long been fighting prejudice, and we have been in the fight.

Does it come as a surprise to you? The modern fight against prejudice began at least eight hundred years ago. Have you heard of our spiritual kinsmen, the Waldensians, of the twelfth century, fleeing to the Alps to multiply their free gospel of free worship high in the mountain valleys?

Or have you heard of John of Paris and of Marsilius of Padua taking life in their hands to cry against a mighty opposing system that all power is not in a pope; it is in the people?

You likely know of Dante Alighieri and his *Divine Comedy*, but in 1311 he was also proclaiming a people's peace as the best condition of mankind.

The predawn thunderings of John Wyclif were not silenced even when his long dead body was exhumed for burning.

Perhaps you have heard of the "praying circles of the peasants." Long before Luther they littered the floors of German forests with prayers they must have thought unheard. From thousands of rude huts crude faith sought to pull down God's arm that the chasms between different kinds of men might be filled in.

Luther was afraid of the early Anabaptists. They were too wild for him in their millennial expectations and their social experiments. Later Lutheranism turned savagely against the Muenster New Jerusalem—perhaps justly, who knows? Only in 1935 were the last skeletons of Muenster martyrs taken from their cage against a town spire, but in and through their wild excesses of the heart ran the teaching that common men must have their day. Those who died were our forebears.

Among the myriads of the unknown who died we can still hear the anguished voices of John Huss, chained to the stake; Balthasar Hubmaier ("Salt me well"); Hugh Latimer ("Courage, Master Ridley"); Dr. Ridley (*in manus tuas, Domini*); Miles Coverdale, and thousands of Huguenots in one dread bloody day; and tens of thousands of death fires of the "Holy Inquisition."

Great was their gift. Fiery the death of every one of them. But *morning stars only they were.*

Barons still owned any woman they wanted among their *"paysans."* Farmers still clenched hands full of soil as they swore allegiance to their liege lord. Men rotted in the mines to make the Fuggers rich. No cow or plow belonged to the man who used it. Not even the dead wood of the forest was free for the taking. Men were strangled for killing crippled deer for meat.

A plowman said, "When day breaks, I drive the oxen to the field and must plow a whole field in the day. My boy is hoarse with the cold and shouting. After that I fill the bins, water the cattle, and carry out the dung. Yea, truly this is great labor because I am not free."

Chalk was taken from the earth to mix with flour. Faces lean; they had no strength to drag around. Pits were dug

123

and the dying dragged to them. Wolves found so many bodies on the road they were emboldened to attack the living.

In Tonnere a man was burned because of the kind of flesh he offered for sale, but another man dug up the buried flesh and was burned, too, for eating it. All over the West the writhing protests were mounting, but a French seigneur could still shoot no more than two peasants off his roof for sport if hunting was poor, and could still bathe his tired feet in human blood after a day in the field. Or so the law said.

II

The world could not stay like this. The big guns opened their barrages on the Continent: the Reformation, the French Revolution, Cardinal Ximénez in Spain.

In 1738 an embittered little man who never weighed more than 120 pounds in his life limped home to England from his complete failure as a preacher in the colony of Georgia. Home to an England where there were 160 crimes punishable by hanging—to steal a loaf of bread cost a life—where public hangings were the only public diversions except that a man could get drunk for a penny or "dead drunk for tuppence," the sign said, or he could watch a bearbaiting or see a prostitute rolled down hill in a barrel on Sunday—that was always sporting.

An England of industrial revolution—where little boys

and girls worked fourteen hours a day at the looms, in the mines, or mired in the stinking prisons, or if you were not one of the thousands dying in the Welsh collieries, perhaps you were five years old and waded all day in a hip-deep vat of cattle urine, turning the piles of wool being bleached in the acid. An England of rotting hulks for ships, drowning sailors, debauched poor, cruel neighbors, grasping landlords and factorymen, slaves—white, black, and tormented.

Sick at heart, dead religiously, the little man, John Wesley, went to meet the Moravian Peter Boehler, who had fire in his heart. With Boehler's fire and Luther's *Preface to the Epistle to the Romans* the fire was transferred. The two found Whitefield and went to the streets like flaming giants with their gospel for the common man.

Years later see Wesley at eighty years of age standing at four o'clock in the morning to preach to four thousand miners at Gwennap Pit, and already his own age had been reborn.

The fire spread—as fires do. Whitefield was clamorously received in America. Twenty thousand could hear him in the open air, tall and gaunt against the sky.

Already in America, from English seed, was a people's movement ready for the torch. It boasted five principles, hammered out on the anvil of long travail.

1. The individual soul is competent to deal with God for itself and is responsible for itself before God.

2. The Church is a fellowship of people who have so dealt with God individually and who come into that fellowship by immersion in water after belief.
3. This fellowship, under Christ, of baptized believers governs itself and is responsible to God.
4. Such a fellowship is entirely separate from the state and must ever remain so.
5. The Holy Scriptures provide the full and authoritative standard for all matters of faith and practice. The teaching of Scripture as interpreted by the fellowship under the Holy Spirit is to guide all personal and social belief and action.

Such principles ran directly counter to state churches, infant baptism, taxation for religious purposes, creedalism, and sacramentarianism. Barriers of law were hastily thrown up, but old man Cartwright preached through his cell bars, blood dripping from his whipped hands; bands of believers withdrew to Kentucky's mountains shutting themselves away from the state church of Virginia and, incidentally, from all social progress for decades to come. Under the preaching of Dan Marshall there was a rippling spread of converts in Georgia, where the young Wesley had given up.

The Revolution swept over, and these early Americans swelled the ranks, pastors and all. John Leland, pastor, announced his candidacy for Orange County representative in the Constitutional Convention in Virginia; but when he learned that James Madison supported his principles, he withdrew and Madison's Bill of Rights became the law of the land after long struggle.

In 1820 a church began to protest against the social vice of slavery. It was little Cherokee Baptist Church, Holston Association, in East Tennessee, near the famous beech tree bearing (until about 1940) the famous words: "D. Boone cilled a bar on this tree."

In 1820 in little Jonesboro settlement came the first real anti-slavery newspaper—the Jonesboro *Emancipator*.

It is quite true that in two or three decades the Uncle Toms and Henry W. Beechers of the North along with the Greeleys would thunder loud against slavery, but this was Baptist and in the *South*.

They, with the Methodists, worked at the evangelism of the Negro. Many members were slavers. Communions split over it, great bitterness billowed up, *but there was progress*.

The first white man to help Negroes organize a church in Paducah, Kentucky, was chased out of town, Pastors were fired, congregations split, *but there was progress*.

Race commissions were born—schools, conventions, and societies. Most associations condemned smoking, drinking, and mixed bathing, never seeing the evils of illiteracy, share cropping, and enforced servitude; *but progress was made*.

It is now true that in the South many seminaries of graduate standing no longer deny admission to Negroes.

Progress has been made, but progress is relative. It was

a great improvement when men quit eating their prisoners of war and started making slaves of them. Progress is relative, and there is yet much to do. But the point I am making is: A fight has been made against prejudice, and *we have been in the fight*.

Yet we made our best fight when we were a small persecuted sect struggling for room to exist. We fought best when the prejudice was against us. Now the curse of respectability is upon us, and it sounds so lovely what our fathers did. While today, as when they carried the corpse of King Henry past the Lady Anne, "O Gentlemen, see, see, dead Henry's wounds open their congealed mouths and bleed afresh." And the present-day situation is such that our whole civilization is involved.

The challenge to our civilization in our age is to *learn to live together*. This we must learn or fly apart in pieces. There seems to be no escape. The age must face it, and its only tool is a spiritual one:

The Church of Jesus Christ

In the last message I claimed that the Church of Jesus is constantly up against things too big to be handled. Too often the only thing we Christians do is to call for the benediction and go home.

And we did it. In the face of slavery, drunkenness, vice, crime, war, and mass starvation we did it. God himself cannot help us if we continue to do it in this crisis of *learning to live together*.

III

But the churches of Jesus have stood in many a desert place. Ten thousand bodies whose graves contain Christian symbols have been found outside old Carthage. Each skeleton holds its skull in its lap. Who were these? In what desert place did they stand? See the thousands waiting to dip handkerchiefs in old Cyprian's blood. Hear older Polycarp crying from his funeral fire, "Eighty-six years have I served Him!"

Hear Savonarola shouting to the Florentians to "pull the cloak of righteousness over your heads before I hail all over you," though his death chains rattled even then.

Have you heard the death cry of that early English translator of the Scriptures: "O God, open the eyes of the King of England"?

Or Luther sending word that he would come to Worms if the very shingles of the roof top turned to devils from hell?

And Cranmer burning off the hand with which he had once signed a retraction of his Protestantism before he allowed the Catholic flames to have the rest of his body?

And the Bishop of Norway, binding his Nazi guards with the chains of the Christ way, so that he could escape to lead his people against Quisling's kind in Norway?

The Church has stood in many desert places. And stands there now. Indeed, this is a desert too. I went apart and wept months ago when I read great Winston

Churchill's speech at Dover. "We will strive forward," he said, "toward that fair future for all men in all the lands . . . *which we thought we had won*, but of which we will never despair."

Which we thought we had won!

I know of a warden in Georgia, and a jury in South Carolina. I know about salt in the soup at Rochester, and no red men in white men's graves in Iowa. I saw a Jew berate a Negro porter for trying to help him in the airport at Knoxville. I have heard about bombs in Dallas and mobs in Cicero. I have seen bedraggled white children sitting on curbs outside movie palaces and grocery stores. I saw GIs turned away from shoddy hovels because they had children. I've watched the "line-up" in police courts on Monday morning, and I have ridden in squad cars on Sunday nights. I know about drunk Mexicans, and hungry sneak thieves, and the powerful clause "Caucasian only" in deeds and contracts. I know about the 284 little sects in America with bigoted little men sniping at each other from behind flimsy little theological ramparts made up of unexamined concepts.

And the societies for the preservation of established prejudices, and the orders for the prolongation of perverted perspectives. I know how important it is not to be an immigrant. How vital it is to have two ancestors of officer rank in the Revolution. How much it helps to resurrect a forgotten coat of arms. How good to have come from Virginia, or to have made Phi Beta Kappa, or to have married money.

I know about railroad tracks and inheritances, share croppers and tenants. I have heard Black Maria's scream as she roared down Madison to pick up a load of flotsam. I have heard the "thwack" as a club met a head outside where I preached in the slums. I have smelt the fourth floor of a broken-down tenement—and I tell you, my Master did not intend *this*.

Whatever Jesus intended, it was not *this*. We have heard; we have known; we have seen and smelt and felt. Our Master did not intend this. *Our brother's blood crieth out from the ground*.

The world waits, and waiting, grows old; and for what does the world wait?

For the manifestation of the sons of God. For the sons of God to *demonstrate themselves*. For the sons of God to *show what they've got*. For the sons of God to *grow up and act like it*.

IV

I believe our hope lies in the Church. I still believe most frankly that our best hope for immediate progress lies in the Church in the South. It is closer to more basic problems. It is able better to understand. It is more personally involved. Its segregation has been more open. Its conscience hurts more keenly. And its progress has been greater.

States like Arkansas and Mississippi have made real progress. Newspapers, notably in Raleigh, Atlanta, Memphis, and Louisville, are leading out. Commissions and committees and schools have been working. But our churches?

It is a desert place, and the Church is not
what my Master intended His Church to be.

For:

The Church was never meant to be a gathering of smug saints.

It is no club for people of proper social standing. It has no valid educational requirements, no set of heraldry and lineage qualifications. That we know, but subtly and with unreasoning power a type of *moral smugness*, the worst of all, has begun to possess us.

I do not forget the dowager leader of a distant church who invited a nine-year-old girl not to come back because her sister had been caught sinning in the town near by.

I do not forget the presiding officer of a woman's society who flounced from a bus in a moral huff, then twenty minutes later had to introduce the main speaker for her society in the person of the Negro she had refused a seat on the bus. The Church must open its eyes.

The Church was not meant to serve as a seedbed for prejudice.

Wherever it is that children learn to be little white, American, Southern provincials; wherever they learn that to be thus is to be thrice-blessed of Jehovah; wherever they learn that ours is always right and best, biggest and purest, and the only right one—wherever they learn it, *let it not be in the Church.*

Teachers, I plead, do not teach my little girls this. They have only begun to suspect it. Don't teach them *that* in church. The Church must produce better fruit.

Nor was the Church meant to serve as a sop to soak up shallowness.

Religion attracts shallow minds as well as deep minds. Jews still require a sign. It is part of our human curse. It was not meant that a big smile and a bear handshake qualified you for religious leadership. Clergymen were not meant to be "props of virtue" breathing a sort of "divine donkeyism" for the comfort of shallow minds. It ought not cost a man his reputation as a Christian if he trains his mind.

Intelligence is not a synonym for heresy. Big numbers are not the equivalent of spiritual victory. Traditional phraseology cannot guarantee a true theology. Pious preachment is no real badge of character. Familiar religious songs do not assure that worship will happen. Last century's standards are not this century's goals. The Church must deepen its channels.

The Church, whatever it is, was never meant to be a fat old lady, sitting in her rock-walled castle, counting war bonds.

Peering out darkened windows at the raucous ribaldry going on in the world outside; building her walls thicker while spiritual chaos rules the homes beyond her walls; spending her energy accumulating her building-fund shekels at the cost of missions and little churches. Leeching on to her select group of socially acceptable hangers-on from whom she mulcts financial support for selfish absorption.

The Church is not a hostess—*she is a serving maid*.

The Church is not a dowager queen—*she is a working girl*.

The Church is no society ruler—*she is a waitress*.

For the Church is not proprietor or even guest—

She is the working handmaid of the Lord.

The Church, like her Master, should be as one that serves; but, as John Oman says, most often she has been as one that sits at meat, for my Master intended the Church to be

A place where men of God were so close together that marvelous things could happen.

Oh, thus will He deal with our prejudices! We are to be men in whom something wonderful has come to pass. We are to be restored to our place as spiritual changers of the world and its prejudices on the basis of the experience we have shared. "God has done something in me," and I am no longer conscious of differences because of the Lord I share with my brothers.

"We are Christians," says Angus, "because we have made our response to a great redeeming act and love which constrains us to be redemptive persons as He was redemptive." We are in the fellowship within which marvelous things can happen.

Do you remember how Simon Peter in Lloyd Douglas' *The Robe* came to see the slave of the Roman patrician when a little girl sent for him? Death had already begun its work in the body of Demetrius, sore wounded for his Master. The huge body of Simon loomed up in the shadows, his bulk towering over the others as he came into the room.

He emptied the slave's bedroom of all save himself and Demetrius. Prostrate he lay, calling on God to save the slave for the sake of the master, for the slave's sake, for Simon's sake, and for the sake of the oneness he, Simon, had with God. And a marvelous thing happened. Demetrius was made well! For God and man were close together, and wonderful things could happen.

Again, my master intended the Church to be *a place where men were so taken with Jesus, so much in love with Him, that they were incapable of littleness and narrowness and selfishness.*

This was the one desire the aged little pastor at Roudaire had for his flock. With heaviness of heart the old priest went to receive the drowned bodies of two illegitimates—a brother and a sister. The one a hugely misshapen gnome, driven to his suicide by the unchristian taunts of the pastor's flock; the other his fairylike sister, who had no reason to go on living in a world that had tormented to

135

death the one thing she loved and had supported by selling her body.

Pierre van Paassen describes the poignant scene when the old man, heartbroken at his people's failure to catch Christ, defied all the laws of his church by bringing the unregenerate bodies of suicide "woods colts" into his sanctuary. Then he sent for all the people to come to the funeral.

This, as I recall it, was the old man's sermon:

In that day, that great day, when the Lord of all shall say to me, "Pasteur de la Roudaire, where are thy sheep?" I shall not answer Him.

And if He shall say to me the second time, "Pasteur de la Roudaire, where are thy sheep?" I shall not answer Him.

But if He shall say to me the third time, "Pastor of Roudaire, I gave thee sheep to guard, where are thy sheep?" then, I shall hang my head and weep, and I shall say, "They were not sheep, O Lord—they were a pack of wolves."

Again, my Master intended his Church to be *a place where men became so humble that all pride of position and race would fall away and the Brotherhood could happen.*

"We talk of putting Him first," says Paul Scherer, "and take to ourselves much unction. Do you suppose it matters? He is first, no matter where we put Him."

And under Him is the Brotherhood where there is room only for humility.

Old Bishop Bienvenu knew that the night he took in

the great dark thief, Jean Valjean, escapee from a slave galley. He knew it, that brotherhood is everywhere.

And he remembered it again the next morning when the gendarmes returned the thief to the bishop along with all the silver Valjean had stolen from his host.

"Good, my boy, you are back! Here, you forgot the candlesticks I gave you with the rest."

That night late passers-by heard anguished sobs coming from the shadows of the church. Jean Valjean was weeping out his heart because after twenty years someone had treated him as a man and a brother.

Finally, my Master intended His Church to be *a place where men became so much like Jesus that people would think they had seen Him.*

A little band of men prayed all year to be like Jesus. At Eastertime the people said that in the cathedral at Milan, as they prayed, they saw wounds come in their hands and feet, and that when a tunic swung apart, they could see a spear wound in a side.

So they called the monks stigmata since they bore the marks of Jesus.

In *The Tree of Liberty* the hero, Matt Howard, tried all his life to be like Washington, because once as a lad he had stopped in the deep Virginia mud to watch young Colonel Washington go by on a beautiful black mare; and as he passed, had caught his pale blue eyes long enough to feel, "Aye, there's a man I can follow till the day I die!"

I do not have it yet; nor do my people have it. A place where we are so close to Him and each other that our selfishness is gone, and our prejudices evaporate, and our brotherhood appears, and we begin to *look like Him.*

I do not have it yet, but I want it, for me and mine. And if my people do not want it, if they cannot abide my wanting it, then are there still brooks and ravens and widows' cruses of oil for those who want it and will come apart to take it. In proportion as the Church of Christ wants it, "a mighty healing is at work in the land."

HERITAGE

CHAPTER NINE

Man is free!
    Freedom is true! And the first of
All gospels is this,
                A lie cannot endure
              forever!
Can we not learn it;
    have we not bitterly relearned it?
Those who died in Argonne Forest did not fail;
Those who did not return from the salient at
Saint-Mihiel have not really died;
Those who lie unmarked in Belgium,
        or smashed on Bataan,
         or gone in the bottom of the sea,
      they did not die unknown,
    if their countrymen remember this:

Our stewardship is that the voice of
little men be not lost.

                Lord God of Hosts, be with us yet.

HERITAGE

I

It is passing strange that our heritage should cost most of us nothing—and some of us everything.

There is a saying among men who have been in battle—common to men from the battles of all ages, Philippi or Waterloo, Valley Forge or Shiloh, Meuse-Argonne, Tarawa, or Yangdok—they say, these veterans say, *"I am old, older than God."*

They mean no sacrilege, no disrespect for God. It is their way of saying that no *young* man ever comes out of battle—all veterans are old. "There is nothing new for us," they mean to say. "We have seen all of it."

141

These are they who keep rebuying our heritage—for our heritage must be rebought, continually.

It is for these men who feel old—"older than God"; these who go forth like Ulysses, "part of all that [they] have met"; for these who, forgotten men of so-called World War I, still carry the stench of death in their nostrils, know yet the cloying pull of the mud in their dreams; for these, and all veterans of all the battles, and for all those who go on waiting for such aged men to return—it is for these that I, who have no right to speak, must yet speak.

Much too much has been said and written in behalf of these who have fought and for whom we wait. The general impression gained from such speaking and writing is

that every man who has ever left home on such a mission is a knight-errant on a white horse swinging a sword of righteousness;

that every man who fought (for our side) is buoyed up by flaming principles that light a faith in him which does not care for death;

that every man who has died and will die (for our side) has gone the way of martyrs, has died the noble death of sacrifice for truth and has become a crucified immortal only a grade lower than the Redeemer.

Such is not the impression one gets whose reading matter is the hearts of those who have returned.

Rather, men go out from home because they must; men fight and die to whom principle may mean nothing and to whom life means *everything;* men meet death in the dirt with no time to think of sacrifice, or crucifixion, or salvation.

And the sadder fact remains in this heritage—denying, moral two-timing, self-centered, buck-passing, mink-coated, five-per-centing, faction-led, rule-by-influence, day-of-government-by-crony—of this mighty land of Greathearts

that I, who have shed no blood,

    I, who have hitherto kept too silent,

    I, who have not lifted up my voice to
cry aloud of the rape of my land by selfish little people,

    I, who have kept my vote and my silence
am not worth one drop of their death blood.

And whose death are you worth?

It is to the task of becoming more nearly worthy of these deaths that have been preserving our heritage; it is to the task of making ourselves more nearly fit to live with these who have returned that we now must set ourselves.

II

Men speak too glibly of freedom; too easily it is mouthed by those who paid nothing for it.

Freedom—beautiful word—Anglo-Saxon word, if you please.

When the French said it, they had to use three words—
liberté, égalité, fraternité.

When the Romans said it, they said only "liberty"
and meant it for Romans only.

When the Greek states tried it, is was for patricians
only.

You have heard that "the Greeks have a word for it."
They have no word for our kind of freedom; their freedom was for royal people, not slaves and commoners.
They have no word for it; there is not even the letter
f in their alphabet.

But the ancient Saxon knew it. He called it *vrai-doom*—
free to choose the cause and the battle, and "free" meant
"all in the family, not a slave." To him it meant that
der mensh in sich, man in himself, is *somebody.*

In Rome, Greece, Athens, Sparta, all freedom was
derived from position in society. Only in the wild North
was freedom *inherent* in the fact that a man was a man.

In all others freedom was deduced, derived, passed
out by society. *Only among the ancient and dreaded
Northerners was it something a man had by divine right.
Free doom*, he said, and meant it.

This concept of freedom, *in the man himself*, is true.
It came to us an ancient inheritance. Of the two hundred billion people who have lived on this earth less
than one billion have had any conception of what freedom means. But man is to be free, that is true. Free in

himself, it is a right of man; and where it is denied him, *it becomes a might of man.*

Man is free! Freedom is true! And the first of all gospels is this, that a lie cannot endure forever. Freedom is true, and a lie cannot endure. So fell the mess that was France in the Revolution.

For man is not free to own the souls of other men, to shoot peasants for pastime if hunting is poor, to knock workmen from housetops with arrows for sport, to deny bread to those who have reaped it.

So fell France. For when Louis XVI thought by subterfuge to deny a meeting place to the National Assembly, they met in a tennis court and swore to an oath that shook all France, burned the Bastille, and took the head of a king.

Man is free, and a lie cannot endure forever.

So fell the colonial system of Britain, for man is free. It is not meant for him to be subject for the benefit of a government. His government is to be for the benefit of the sovereign, man himself.

Man is free, and a lie cannot endure forever.

So fell the institution of slavery in America, and in Brazil, and in British possessions. For man is free. He cannot be owned by other men, and a lie cannot endure forever.

So fell the national socialism and the Fascism of Hitler and Benito. For man is free, and a lie cannot endure.

Socialism and Fascism are lies, and Adolf and Benito went down to their private hells, for man is free.

And so one day will fall Communism, for it too is a lie, bred of the great lie about economic determinism and earthly bread; for lies cannot endure forever. Man is free.

Freedom—beautiful word!

Word that needs no qualification.

We speak of freedom *of* and freedom *from*. I am a great deal more interested in freedom *by* dint of my own sacrificial devotion to the truth that man is free.

These qualifying phrases are not needed in the pure concept of freedom. Freedom is not qualified, not a matter of degrees. No man is partly free. He is free, or he is not free.

It is a perfect word. Free or bound. We believe in freedom *of* religion, *of* conscience, *of* work and enterprise, *of* the press, *of* opinion. We long for freedom *from* fear, *from* want, *from* oppression. But all these things are gathered up in the word itself—*freedom*.

Freedom, Anglo-Saxon word, means "all in the family." The family gathers up all the "of's" and "from's," for a man is in or he is out.

The war has taught us, as Carlyle long ago said, that the same leaky bottom in these wild waters bears us all; yet we are like the professor at Padua who refused to look through Galileo's telescope at the true world— afraid of what he might learn.

So we, afraid to look into our own concepts of freedom, are afraid that we might find that we do not truly believe in freedom; for it means all in the tribe, all in the family, all in the race—the *human race*.

As Reinhold Niebuhr puts it so effectively, "All human life is involved in the sin of seeking security at the expense of other life." This is our corporate evil.

III

In our defense of freedom we are directed to look here, and there, and there, and there, for the enemy. Actually he is closer. Cromwell, having his wounds dressed during the battle of York, heard that the Earl of Manchester and his army had fled the field, the battle lost. He found the earl with his staff, dashing headlong from the field. "My Lord," he cried, "you mistake the road; the enemy is not there."

The enemy is not there, nor there, nor there; he is here in me, in you—in any of us where freedom is denied.

To be free means to be "in the family." In the face of the denied freedoms of this earth I cannot join these modern panegyrists who pitch the note of admiration upward and higher until they are screaming in falsetto.

I join Lin Yutang in saying that I do not believe in any automatic millennium that is going to blossom out of this spiritual desert. I smell too many corpses around.

For peace on earth is an act of faith, and without

147

faith we shall not be saved. It happens that we are a generation almost without faith. I keep remembering how bitter we poor mortals have made this earth for each other. There are sections of any city through which a sensitive man riding must weep.

On the other hand, in the Southland there is high hope. I came from the same clay as did my hearers. Their prejudices are mine, and we fight them with the same tools. Those of us who are fighting our own prejudices rejoice that there are judges, that there are teachers, pulpits, great newspapers in great metropolitan areas, and hosts of ordinary believers who will yet see the Southland rid itself of its littleness in the matter of resentment of difference—whether in religion or race.

There is hope. Nature herself will help us. God himself will guide us. For through all the centuries nature has gone on insisting that men shall be born with all their transcendental longings incorrigibly active.

Men still desire freedom, and one day *it will come*. God help us! Some day we will grow beyond patriotism, beyond nationalism, beyond backyards, to our heritage for *all the sons of earth*.

Some day—

> Surely by Will, he will blow clear,
> His trumpets that all ears shall hear,
> And helping angels shall sweep near
> And the banners of the soul advance,

Up, out of hate and ignorance,
Into a new inheritance.[1]

IV

Men speak too glibly of freedom. Too easily it is
mouthed by those of us who paid nothing for it. We
must come to see that *any* heritage brings an attendant
responsibility. We must come to understand that *nations
as nations have a stewardship over their heritage.*

The rubbish heap of history receives all nations who
lose sight of the responsibility for their inheritance. God
gives no gift for the receiver's exclusive use. Any gift
from Him brings responsibility. When any nation re-
fuses the responsibility, *it rejects the heritage.* And a
disinherited nation dies.

The rubbish heap of nations is piled high.

Greece, with its genius for culture, first to catch the
high spirit of Man, yet wanted what she caught to be
Greek man and Greek culture; and Greece died while
Hellas lived in other peoples.

Israel, with an inborn capacity for God, with her
genius for religion above all other peoples, yet drowned
herself in her own nationalism, keeping God a Jew
while Jehovah sent a cosmic Christ.

Persia, genius of metaphysical thought, land of the
light and the eternal, preferred a Persian Light; but her

[1] From John Masefield, *A Letter from Pontus, and Other Verse.*
Copyright 1936 by The Macmillan Company and used with their
permission.

149

great god Mazda has become an electric light bulb, "guaranteed."

Rome, greatest among governors and lawyers, most able among organizers and empire builders, Rome, the believer in justice, yet believed only in Roman justice, Roman law, Roman empire, and Roman unity.

And it was so that around A.D. 410 a wild "longbeard" from the North thrust his spear up the nostril of the Roman goddess of justice and turned over the Roman boundary god, Terminus. But the gods did not resent it.

Rome was dead—and Pax Romana sounds like a new dairy feed, and the might premise *vox populi, vox Dei* has become a radio show called *Vox Pop.*

Great Britain, logical successor to Rome (for neither the Holy Roman nor the Spanish empires had the seeds of greatness and high purpose to qualify as Rome's successor), has had a genius for empire, and hardship, and expansion. With her comparatively clear grasp of much of the Reformation and her claims to "Christian" bases for expansion, in spite of evil and cruelty of method, she had frequently in her leaders a sense of stewardship, a sense of destiny and possessions held in trust. For three hundred years, often in spite of herself, she was the chief secular factor in the expansion of Christianity.

But the empire is a-dying—or dead. The age of empire is done for. Imperialism is no part of God's way for this age. The world must govern itself, and the commonwealth of nations is not an empire. Men must govern themselves, not be governed.

We call it the "democratic principle," and that brings us to the *stewardship of America*.

Four hundred and fifty years ago the plain men of this earth began to take over. Everywhere in Europe Man as Man was stirring—crying for his place in the sun as Somebody, tired forever of the enslaving, denying, unworthy cuttings of a system built for a few, tired to death of the endless agony of denied manhood.

Man was stirring, stirring for his matchless march, the march of common men to freedom.

In the *North* the bound bull that was Germany roared, and he roared in the voice of Martin Luther, greater than Bismarck would be, as he hammered in his rough German to Germans for Germans about Germany and Christ.

In *France* the teachings of certain "heretics" like John of Paris and Abelard had begun to have their effect, and the peasantry was tiring of oppression.

In *Spain*, the power of Ferdinand and Isabella had made a world empire built on a pyramid of protesting slaves.

And in *England* already there was Magna Charta, and in a while there would be a Cromwell and later a Wesley and a Shaftesbury, to relieve sailors from death traps, little boys from the mines and the acid pits of wool bleachers, and the rabble from the gallows' 160 major crimes.

Yet *Man could not come into his own in Europe.* Somehow in the providence of God to Europeans was opened a wide, rich, new land—unknown, comparatively unoccupied. It was suddenly thrown open to the gaze of men 450 years ago. And it had a most astounding effect on history. A new life was possible. The old life was impossible in the new land, for none of its trimmings were available. It was a time of demand for discovery, enlightenment, and development. Here was the seedbed.

Now, four hundred years later, seed from the seeds the old world sent is blowing back. And men from Santa Barbara to the St. Lawrence have contrasted all over the world what it means to be free. They are seeing as we must see:

Democracy is our stewardship.

The right of the individual is our heritage.

The blood of martyrs has ever been seed. From Valley Forge to Terracina it ever calls out from the ground.

This way, land of ours, *forget not your heritage*, your stewardship. Therein only lies your power, *the hope you hold out for "little men."*

Can we not learn it; have we not bitterly learned it? Those who died in Argonne Forest did not fail; those who did not return from the salient at Saint-Mihiel have not really died; those who lie unmarked in Belgium, or smashed on Bataan, or gone in the bottom of the sea,

they did not die unknown *if Americans remember this:*
Our stewardship is that the voice of little men be not
lost.

> If, drunk with sight of power, we loose
>   Wild tongues that have not Thee in awe,
> Such boasting as the Gentiles use
>   Or lesser breeds without the law:
> Lord God of Hosts, be with us yet,
> Lest we forget, lest we forget! [2]

[2] From: *The Five Nations*, by Rudyard Kipling. Copyright 1903 by Rudyard Kipling, reprinted by permission of Mrs. George Bambridge and Doubleday & Company, Inc.

CHAPTER TEN

The show never changes.
    Only the actors change.
        Even the scenery is the same.

Bloody Teutoburger!
    Varus is dead, Augustus.
        And Patton, the brilliant, too.

But there is no peace.
    This morning I learned to spell new words—
        Pyongyang,
            Yangdok,
                Wonsan—strange-sounding foreign words.

They tell me they have buried in the Orient a kid I married in my parlor not two months ago. And the Seventh Marines, with the Twenty-fourth, Second, and Twenty-fifth Divisions of the Eighth Army, didn't know when Christmas passed, for though "man is where nature and spirit meet," there is trouble in Korea.

IS THERE NO PEACE?

Mid-Century:

Mankind's sprawling procession of good, bad, learned, ignorant, plenty-laden, and poverty-ridden plods down a long road with no visible turning. Long centuries trailing their ghost processions behind; new centuries clamoring in the distance for their birth.

The little fat boys grown up to clutch their useless hoardings; the self-centered little girls made mothers, only to twist their real life baby dolls out of form and shape; the broken and mangled, the maimed and woebegone, begrimed by their journey—

These sear the seeing heart at Christmastime. It was not meant so to be.

Mid-Century:

This "so-called" twentieth century—all the ghosts of man's glory and degradation calling out to the seeing heart,

"There is no automatic progress."

It is not enough to walk in the procession. Human personality was meant to be *well*, but it must earn its *wellness*.

Mid-Century:

"Only historians make divisions; time never does." It's all the same line of march—but not to automatic victory. Man was meant to walk like man and never to sprawl. Yet only Divine Personality can lead into the road that needs no turning place.

The victory of peace can never be an automatic accomplishment for the race of persons, and yet personality itself can never be utterly routed. Only the Man Personality can triumph and he only as he follows the will of the Divine Personality.

Mid-Century:

And there is no peace on this long road. It was not meant so to be. For they called Him "Prince of Peace" once upon a time.

156

I

Eighteen centuries later a distinguished Briton began his now classic rebuttal in the Parliament by crying, "The gentleman's cry is for peace, but there is no peace." Still later by a hundred years in a special school for refugee children a fourteen-year-old girl was asked to draw a picture of her earlier home as she remembered it. She drew a better picture than she knew when on the board she scrawled a hopelessly confused disconcatenation of meaningless strokings. She had no home. There had been for her no home. There was no peace for her. There had been no peace for her land.

There is no peace. There never has been peace. Not in two thousand years of Christian history has there been peace.

Even while the angels sang their "Laudamus Te" to the newborn Prince of Peace—even then a German war lord was sending a word to Caesar: "Send your vaunted Roman legions against me if you dare; I shall teach them what my axmen who have not slept under roof for fourteen years can do."

Not very long before the resurrection of that Prince of Peace, a Roman emperor, the great one, Augustus Imperator, was running insanely around the balustrade of his palace, crying as he ran, "O Varus, Varus! Give me back my legions." But the legions of Varus never came back. The bones of forty thousand crack legionnaires bleached in Teutoburger Forest along with the bones of their general, Varus. They had met those ax-men close to where other legions would meet them twenty centuries later in still another "Battle of the Bulge."

Almost before the gospel of peace had time to cross the Dardanelles and get a start into Europe, even then the blood of dead Jews was hock deep on Roman horses in Jerusalem's gutters. Titus had taken her, taken Jerusalem "like a hut in a cucumber field" as a coronation present for his former commander, the new emperor, Vespasian, his father.

While Leo, greatest of the Roman bishops, was preaching universal peace, peace for all men in the world, even while he preached, Attila and his 750,000 hungry Huns stormed the gates of Rome, the City Eternal, Capital of Empire.

Across the Mediterranean Sea a man was forging out some mighty spiritual weapons for his generation and those to follow. He spoke of the *City of God* and made a book called *Confessions*. But even as Augustine was writing, "*O Lord, Thou hast made us for Thyself, and our hearts are restless until they find their rest in Thee,*" even then, while Augustine was writing, the Vandal hordes of Genseric, conquerors of Spain and North Africa, were beating down the gates of Hippo, where Augustine was writing. There is no peace.

The generation that began when Gregory the Great

sent his first missioner to the wilds of Angleland saw before its close the release of a wild torrent of slaughter in the East—hundreds of thousands of insanely religious sons of Islam, screaming their *Lo'Illah Il Allah* as they burned and raped and converted.

While Alcuin, princely prince of education in the court of Charlemagne, was making Aachen the center of learning and preaching, compiling his great collection of sermons for ignorant priests to use, even then with priests at his side Charlemagne was sending fifty-five major military expeditions out of that same Aachen; and *at the same spot where his priests baptized four thousand Saxons at the Weber River, the great Charlemagne cut off four thousand Saxon heads* on his way home.

In the early years of the twelfth century the saintly Bernard sang:

> Jesus, the very thought of Thee
> With sweetness fills the breast;
> But sweeter far Thy face to see,
> And in Thy presence rest.

Even then 300,000 men and 10,000 children died in empty crusade; Norsemen, Magyars, and the wolves that came out of Asia ravaged all of France; and William the Conqueror, falling in the mud as he landed at Hastings, had put his muddy hands on England's throat fifty years before.

While Dante, immortal peacemaker, wrote of the best

possible condition of man—a people's peace—it was not a long generation away that John Huss, Bohemian, would back up to his stake in Constance for the sake of the Name; and already German gates were shuddering at the blows of Mohammedan hammers; Spain was in her eternal, internal turmoil; Constantinople was falling; the Crusades had failed; and Britain was more a set of warring tribes than a nation.

While the great Cardinal Ximénez was reforming Spanish Catholicism and blessing all mankind with his reconstruction of the Greek New Testament, Pizarro and Cortés were converting Indians to the faith by choking their kings to death, and the emperor of the Germans was fighting three wars at the same time. Man is a contradiction. There is no peace.

For Luther, whose Ninety-five Theses gave Mankind a freedom he had never known, wrote also *Against the Murderous and Thieving Hordes of Peasants.*

The Calvin who gave us the *Institutes* had much to do with the burning of Servetus, who as a physician traced the course of blood in the human body, but as an amateur theologian had his blood turned to steam in his veins for denying the Trinity right in Calvin's Geneva. And the same age sang the terrible Sicilian Vespers, watched the drowning of ten thousand Anabaptists and Mennonites, and smelt the smoke of the flaring death fires for a hundred years. There isn't any peace.

But the story is different now, you say. Look at the great and peaceful expansion of Christianity in modern times. The age of William Carey and Adoniram Judson, Hudson, Yates, and Duff.

And still there is no peace. For within the hundred years Great Britain fought Germany, France, Spain, and the thirteen colonies twice; Napoleon ravaged Europe; and the Germans captured Paris.

In the decade when China was just beginning to open to Christianity, Great Britain was wrestling the Bear for the Crimea, and my people were fighting my people at Shiloh and Murfreesboro, Franklin and Chattanooga.

In 1914 the kingdom of God was just around the corner, men said, but in the heat of war the Calvinist Presbyterian head of one great nation had to send a million men into the heart of another nation headed by a Kaiser just as Calvinist (Reformed) as he. It was a war to end war. But men had never heard, then, of Wake and Tarawa, and Dunkirk, and the hedgerows, and Teutoburger Forest, where we came in.

The show never changes.

Only the actors change.

Even the scenery is the same.

Bloody Teutoburger!

Varus is dead, Augustus.

And Patton, the brilliant, too.

There is no peace.

This morning I learned to spell new words—
Pyongyang,
    Yangdok,
        Wonsan—strange-sounding foreign words.
They tell me they have buried in the Orient a kid I married in my parlor not two months ago. And the Seventh Marines, with the Twenty-fourth, Second, and Twenty-fifth divisions of the Eighth Army, didn't know when Christmas passed, for "though man is where nature and spirit meet," there is trouble in Korea.

Thus far in Man's rapid run the wild turbulence of nature's raw torrents has completely swallowed the deeper tranquillity of the spirit and its dream. For man—cruel, heartless, empty—strips to the barbaric, strips his boasted civilization like a shell, every time a brass horn blows.

Masefield saw it—after the days when men had learned to spell Meuse-Argonne, Saint Mihiel, Château-Thierry—and wrote "The Wild Geese":

.   .   .   .

> They have no masses, no classes,
> No wars, no poison-gasses,
> They are geese, they are asses.
>
> O, it must be absurd
> To be a goose of a bird
> And salute no general spurred.
> Civilization rots,
> When men aren't killed with shots.

Souls grow rustic and mothic
Unless kept cut-throat and gothic;

If we could put goose-brain
In airship or aeroplane,
We could drop bombs like rain.
Make such holes in the mud,
Fill them full with such blood,

Give God thanks for security,
Practice Racial Purity,
And be (if God should please),
Almost as wise as geese.[1]

There is no peace.

> *And in despair I bowed my head;*
> *"There is no peace on earth," I said;*
> *"For hate is strong, and mocks the song*
> *Of peace on earth, good will to men!"*

II

> *Then pealed the bells more loud and deep:*
> *"God is not dead, nor doth he sleep!*
> *The wrong shall fail, the right prevail,*
> *With peace on earth, good will to men!"*

In this din of war a-borning, I say it, there has always been peace.

[1] From John Masefield, *A Letter from Pontus, and Other Verse.* Copyright 1936 by The Macmillan Company and used with their permission.

There is peace now—

in the face of broken pacts and disrupted conferences, in the face of new draft quotas and U.N. vetoes, in the face of those who remember dead Arabs and Jews, the bodies of guerrillas without heads.

There is peace now—

with blazing red banners in Milan and Paris, Rome and China, all Asia gone Red—even before the pitiable "Banzai!" uttered by miserable Togo from his little Buddhist chapel en route to gallows has died away.

There is peace now—

with the wounded streaming by air and ship into stateside hospitals from that thinning circle of glorious Marines holding their perimeter against the Asian flood, red flood; even with them

there is peace—

a strange kind of peace that comes and makes a garrison out of a man's heart.

Six months after the shattering of Rommel's Desert Corps I got it. It had started its way to me from an ordinary foxhole on a desert hillside where a division of scared, marvelously brave kids from Indiana and Texas, Kansas and Alabama, were pinned down by German fire. Their pitiably thin armor not built for the fire of eighty-eight millimeter guns, they had lain there all day taking the first real blasting of their lives. As a chaplain crawled along the line of holes, a long-jawed boy from a Northern state flipped it to him, crying, "Hey, Chappie, mail that for me, will ya?"

Months later I got it. Sacred to the memory of a boy I had seen find his Christ, I keep it with my best-loved things to make me remember—with the dirt of Africa smeared, my name crudely misspelled, but the message was plain enough:

"I want to trust Him again and let you know I've lived for Him and will some more if I get the chance," and a name.

There has always been peace—peace that comes and makes a garrison out of a man's heart.

But peace has never been national; peace has never been external. Peace has never been act or deed. Peace is not even a goal. Peace is never achievement. Peace is not even a contracted agreement.

Peace is individual—not national. Peace is internal—not external. Peace is attitude—not act. Peace is result—not goal. Peace is inheritance—not achievement. Peace is a spiritual operation—not a condition. Peace is a way of life—not a contracted agreement. *Peace,* I say, *is individual.*

To make the rain fall in times of drought some primitive peoples used to send their magicians up in trees with buckets of water. Their function was to pray, with incant and descant, wildly and loudly and long, while between cries they tipped their buckets to spill a little water down to prime the pumps of heaven and make it rain. But rain doesn't come that way. And neither does peace. Though our magicians have met from Dumbarton Oaks to Paris, from San Francisco to London to Potsdam, the buckets have been thoroughly tipped— are well-nigh empty—but peace doesn't come that way, and neither does rain. Rain comes up from the earth in droplets, individual droplets drawn by the warming sun, before the drops descend to earth as rain. And so does peace. The waters of peace come up like the dew from the ground, where even the grains of sand are individual.

Peace is a matter for individuals. It has always been a matter for individuals. It can become a matter for nations only as it becomes a reality for individuals. How can there be peace between *nations* when there is no peace in the *state*, and how can there be peace in the *state* before there is peace in the *county*, and how a peaceful *county* without a peaceful *town*, and how peace in my *town* until there is peace in my *church?* And how, pray, is there to be peace in my *church* until there is peace in *me?* And how can there be peace in *me* until I have gone to the *Source of peace?*

Peace, I say, *is internal attitude*, not external act.

Peace has never been external. In spite of Pax Romana and Pax Britannica it is inside, or it isn't. Peace is internal. No society can survive the chaos that is produced when its members treat each other as they treat other groups. The trick is to learn to treat other groups like we must treat each other in a peaceful society. But it begins

166

within. A man wouldn't survive five minutes in some sections of our society if he acted as an individual toward his neighbors as some of us have acted toward other denominations and nations. And who could survive if he treated his next-door neighbor as he was taught to behave toward Germans and Japanese?

Hear me! *What we call holy will not survive another fifty years of our treating each other as nations treat other nations.* Peace must come from inside.

Peace is internal, not external; and, therefore, is a thing of *attitude* and not *act*. A man can do peace while his inner spirit is treachery, but he cannot do treachery while his inner spirit is peace. One day a man approached his emperor crying, "Ave! Imperator!" and that was an act of peace and a sign of peace—but the inner attitude was not peace, and the next act was a knife in the corpse of Gaius Julius Caesar. The act of peace for Japan was to keep her emissaries dealing with Secretary Cordell Hull in Washington. But there was no peace in spite of acts of peace—for attitude had already determined Pearl Harbor. How easily man is fooled by act! Have you heard what color the atmosphere turned around Cordell Hull's desk that morning in Washington?

Peace is internal before external, attitude before act.

Peace, I say, *is resultant inheritance, not achieved goal; a spiritual operation, not a contracted agreement.*

Peace is result, never goal; an incidental result of a way of life, not a deliberately-to-be-sought end. Peace

167

is inheritance—gift; not achievement—goal. It is the inheritance of the people of the Kingdom. It is *not* the achievement on earth of a unity of worship and dogma. One of the greatest strengths of the Christian frame is that it has been able to develop in so many directions and to appeal to so varied a list of personalities.

Peace never was a matter of getting all the Methodists to unite with all the Baptists. Even before the Nicene Council in A.D. 325, already Christianity had ninety different frames, each of which was heresy to the remaining majority and all of which had some grasp of Jesus at the heart. Peace is a spiritual operation, not a condition of unity. It is an "act of faith" says the Chinese Lin Yutang, but it so happens that we are a generation almost without faith, and without faith who can be saved?

Peace is not something I agree to keep by contract; it is a way to live as the result of something I have received. It is the spiritual operation of faith, not a condition or state. It is neither national, nor external, nor act, nor achievement, nor condition.

On the contrary peace is individual, internal, attitude, inheritance, a lived way. It is something that happens to you as the result of receiving its Source. *It is so wonderful a thing that it is understandable that those who do not have it should seek it and that those who will not receive it should be forced to go without it.*

Christianity according to the teachings of Jesus has never promised world peace except as peace comes from the grass roots up. The world order has never been such that it could be called Christian. The powers that be have never belonged to Him. Always He has worked in spite of them, on the individual grains of sand.

Christianity has never been responsible for producing world peace—for Christianity *is* war.

> God *versus* Mammon
> *Alter versus* Ego
> I *versus* Me
> Good *versus* Ill
> The Man that I could be
> *versus*
> The Man I am.

Christianity is *war*.

War that produces peace the only way war can ever produce peace—by surrender.

Christianity is *divisive*.

The claims of Christ set a man against himself. Once he faces up to the claims of Christ, he is torn, divided, at war, until surrender.

Man can never be justified by his products, new gadgets, nursery-rhyme creeds, one-eyed philosophies, mud-pie civilization, kindergarten councils, like little boys agreeing to freeze no more snowballs and throw no more mud.

Man can only be justified in himself, and his justification begins only when he is a man of peace—and his peace comes only with *surrender to the Source of peace* against which he fights.

Jesus deals with individuals, and this is the key to His peace—giving.

He searches for the point in every man upon which He may lay hold and begin leading him to the kingdom of God. He lays hold of him at the point of his greatest need—dominion of demons, fear of death, fear of life, error, night, sin, perversion, emptiness.

Beginning with a man's lack of peace, beginning where a man is, He leads into the available peace, the kind that passes understanding, that comes and garrisons a man's heart.

Strange, in this warring world—and the most beautiful thing in it—how important this peace is to God.

It is in the advent—

"Peace among men of good will."

God re-enunciates an ageless principle—there has always been peace among men whose hearts are right to each other.

It is in the teaching—

"Blessed are the makers of peace."

Happy are those who have begun to reproduce the peace that indwells and defends a man's heart. I find 31 forms of the word in the Scriptures; I have counted 393 verses where the word is central.

Peace—it is awfully important to Him.

It is in the Death—Ascension—

"Peace I leave with you, my peace I give unto you: not as the world giveth, give I unto you."

But it is in accord with the mind of Jesus and at the same time a fact of history that the gospel peace comes only in connection with a believing surrender to the person of Christ. The Father has promised His peace to such sons—and "because ye are sons," you are above life's disastrous days.

> Oh, well for him whose feet have trod
> The weary road of toil and strife
> Yet from the sorrow of his life
> Builds ladders to be nearer God.

Sons of the Father are beyond disaster.

Carlyle tells Hugo's story of a little bird sitting on the limb of a tree until a stroke of lightning cut the supporting limb from under. The song stopped for the moment, but the bird was unhurt; it had wings, wings to put it above disaster.

But a man has to surrender to get his wings. A man has to surrender as simply as did Simeon the day he met the parents of Jesus, the child, in the temple—and taking the child in his arms, surrendering to the message he received, he sang the immortal "Nunc Dimittis" for all believing hearts:

> "Lord, now permittest Thou Thy servant
>   to go away in peace,

as Thou hast said,
    for these eyes of mine
        have seen *Thy salvation*."

Mid-Century:

And there is no peace on this long road?
Untrue! Untrue!
There has always been peace for the believing
heart—

    He who would valiant be
      'Gainst all disaster,
    Let him in constancy
      Follow the Master.

DEBIT

Any man would be hard pressed if called upon to give credit for borrowed language alone, much less for ideas. The list below is an honest attempt to acknowledge both words and ideas that feel like my own and are not. A reading of these works is infinitely rewarding. These represent my creditors not sufficiently acknowledged even here.

Augustine, *Confessions*
Bell, Bernard Iddings, *God Is Not Dead*
Berdyaev, Nicolas, *The Destiny of Man*
_____, *The Meaning of History*
Bready, John Wesley, *England: Before and After Wesley*
Brunner, Emil, *The Divine-Human Encounter*
_____, *Man in Revolt*
Cochrane, C. N., *Christianity and Classical Culture*
Coulton, G. G., *Medieval Panorama*
Dixon, MacNeile, *The Human Situation*
Dostoevsky, Fyodor, *The Brothers Karamazov*

—————————, *Crime and Punishment*
Harnack, Adolf, *What Is Christianity?*
Kierkegaard, Sören, *The Concept of Dread*
—————————, *The Sickness unto Death*
Latourette, Kenneth S., *The Christian Outlook*
Luther, Martin, *Preface to the Epistle to the Romans*
Niebuhr, Reinhold, *The Nature and Destiny of Man*
Oman, John, *Concerning the Ministry*
Oxnam, G. Bromley, *Preaching in a Revolutionary Age*
Sayers, Dorothy, *Creed or Chaos*
—————————, *A Man Born to Be a King*
Sorokin, Pitirim A., *The Crisis of Our Age*
Wesley, John, *Journal*, I, II

Carver, W. O., lectures on the Expansion of Christiantiy
Davis, W. H., and McDowell, Edward A., lectures in New Testament
    Interpretation
Denman, William, a sermon at Paducah, Kentucky
Luccock, Halford A., special lectures at Southern Baptist Theological
    Seminary
Mackay, John, a sermon at Louisville, Kentucky
Stealey, S. L., lectures in Church History
Tribble, Harold W., lectures in Theology